WINTER SUN / THE DUMBFOUNDING

Margaret Avison
Winter Sun /
The Dumbfounding
Poems 1940-66

The Modern Canadian Poets

McCLELLAND AND STEWART

The Canadian Publishers
McClelland and Stewart Limited
25 Hollinger Road, Toronto M4B 3G2

Canadian Cataloguing in Publication Data

Avison, Margaret, 1918 –
    Winter Sun/The Dumbfounding

(The Modern Canadian poets)

Poems.

ISBN 0-7710-0983-6

I. Title. II. Title: The Dumbfounding. III. Series.

PS8501.V57W66   C811'.54   C82-094871-3
PR9199.3.A92W66

Grateful acknowledgement is made to the Ontario Arts Council for its assistance.

Author's Photo: Newsome Photography
Set in Mergenthaler Sabon by Trigraph Inc., Toronto
Printed and bound in Canada by T.H. Best Printing Co.

Contents

Winter Sun

The Apex Animal

A Horse, thin-coloured as oranges ripened in freight-cars
which have shaken casements through the miles of night
across three nights of field and waterfront warehouses –
rather, the narrow Head of the Horse
with the teeth shining and white ear-tufts:
It, I fancy, and from experience
commend the fancy to your inner eye,
It is the One, in a patch of altitude
troubled only by clarity of weather,
Who sees, the ultimate Recipient
of what happens, the One Who is aware
when, in the administrative wing
a clerk returns from noon-day, though
the ointment of mortality
for one strange hour, in all his lustreless life,
has touched his face.

(For that Head of a Horse there is no question
whether he spent the noon-hour with a friend,
below street-level, or on the parapet –
a matter which may safely rest
in mortal memory.)

All Fools' Eve

From rooming-house to rooming-house
The toasted evening spells
City to hayrick, warming and bewildering
A million motes. From gilded tiers,
Balconies, and sombre rows,
Women see gopher-hawks, and rolling flaxen hills;
Smell a lost childhood's homely supper.
Men lean with folded newspapers,
Touched by a mushroom and root-cellar
Coolness. The wind flows,
Ruffles, unquickens. Crumbling ash
Leaves the west chill. The Sticks-&-Stones, this City,
Lies funeral bare.
Over its gaping arches stares
That haunt, the mirror mineral.
In cribs, or propped at plastic tablecloths,
Children are roundeyed, caught by a cold magic,
Fading of glory. In their dim
Cement-floored garden the zoo monkeys shiver.
Doors slam. Lights snap, restore
The night's right prose.
Gradually
All but the lovers' ghostly windows close.

Dispersed Titles

Through the bleak hieroglyphs
of chart and table
thumb-tacked for winnowed navigators
who stroke the sable air,
earth's static-electric fur,
who ride it, bucked or level,
master it with minerals gouged and fabricated
out of it, insist
on being part of it, gouged out,
denatured nature, subject
to laws self-corrugated,
created out of it,
through these hieroglyphs and chart
mark with the hearing of the eye
the bellrung hours of Tycho Brahe.

He – Kepler's Orpheus –
a Danish crown, the bishops,
the snarling North Sea night,
bakers of biscuit,
ladies, sweet ladies,
stuffed in their cabinets, swollen with toothache,
the straw and bran
unfabling fields already,
while the Narcissus sun
lends clods a shining:
All somewhere, still,
though they seem lost away
from their weird hollow under the solar architrave.

Are they all only in
those other hieroglyphs
of the created, solitary brain?
borne here in a man-toy?
bounced up, a ball
that chooses when to fall,
comets for hap,
a new respect for the extremes?

Something wrought by itself out of itself
must bear its own
ultimates of heat and cold
nakedly, refusing
the sweet surrender.
Old Mutabilitie has been
encompassed too, wrought into
measures of climbing and elipse.
This little fierce fabrique
seals the defiant break
with cycles, for old Tycho Brahe's sake.

But soft! (o curly Tudor) –
no pith of history will
be cratered in one skull.

The continents, my brother Buckminster
no cramp of will comprises.
The oak that cracked a quilted tumulus
and rustled, all through childhood's
lacey candle-drip of winter,
through feathered morning hours, later
through glass, so that the glassy
exultation of an articulate
stripped rock-and-ribs,
an intellect
created into world, was
wounded with whispers from a single oak-tree.

The periwinkle eyes
of seaborde men
too young for gladness
fade with their shanties.
Lost, like the committing of sins,
crag-shapes are sediment,
chopped down, minced, poured to pave the shelving
parade ground for pinioned grotesques
in the pink shadow-lengthening
barracks of evening.

(The earth has other roots and selves)

For Tycho Brahe's sake I find myself,
but lose myself again for
so few are salvaged
in the sludge of the
ancestral singular.

Ancestral? Even my brother
walks under waving plumes of strangeness.
The northern centuries
funnel me, a chute of
steel and water tumbling,
and I forget
warm boards, old market awnings,
the two fat little feet in shawls
treading a beaded woman's easy arm
by a sunned stone,
a ginger root
in a stone jar,
a lattice-work of iron
in a dry wind, overlooking
fuchsia flats and the
scorched Moorish mountains,
or holy peaks frilled with cirrus ice
and the slick-paper blues and greens
of their flanks rich
with floral forest.

(The nameless one dwells in his tents)

Forget much more...
a name, not the made-name
corrupted to man-magic, to fend off
the ice, the final fire of this
defiance.

Things I can't know I smell
as plainly as if invisible campfires
smoked: a hum of sightless suppers
on the iridescent shore
under the dunes. The wanderer's
sandals ship, and shift, cool sand.

(And "up" is a direction)

Because one paces (none, now, strut)
one faces sea and space and is
tempted to think: Proscenium!
We have revolted.

Only the stagestruck mutter still
to the night's empty galleries.
Tossed out in the confused up-and-down
too many have casually
fingered the gilt loge fringes,
snuffed into dust the
desiccated peanut-shells
since the last true audition,
and found not even ghosts even in the echoing foyer.

Chronic

My house is made of old newspapers.
Not very old ones, always about a week's
Accumulation. And don't pretend you recognize it.
You don't. Because it doesn't look like a house,
Either square or tepee-shaped, and *I* wouldn't know
Except it's where I live.
The draughts, the imperfect or too day-bald light,
Even the constant shifting of the contour
Are not, as difficulties, insurmountable.
But as the weeks pass I become accustomed
To failing more and more
In credence of reality as others
Must know it, in a context, with a coming
And going marshalled among porticos,
And peacock-parks for hours of morning leisure.

What with the winter solstice
There is no chance of a strawberry festival
For months. I cannot think . . .
Quinces, for instance: will I need
A pocket-knife for that? I never see, these days,
Even that chap in a peak cap
(Spoke like a Cockney and) surprised us once at Brewster's.

Prelude

The passive comes to flower, perhaps
a first annunciation for the spirit
launched on its seasons.

The turning-point is morning:
now Budapest, now feathery
fields – where explorers' maps showed nothing –
now a crippled crofter's in his doorway or
the Scandinavians' by the sea.

Under the dry fence
gooseberries dangled on thin stems,
cottony grass buried the fence-posts, the
grainy dirt trickled with ants.
I smell bare knees again and summer's clouds.

Somebody's grandpa came
in shirt-sleeves, solid
and asymmetrical, rooting the word
"trunk," for a child, as right
for man or tree.
He stood, and gnarled
silently, while he talked over our heads
to some invisible neighbour
we did not bother glancing up to see.

The honeycombing sun
opened and sealed us in
chambers and courts and crooked butteries,
cities of sense.

Tomes sag on the begrimed shelves
locking in light.

Most men would rather take it straight.
Nothing can contrive
accepting. Sparrows in the curbs

and ditch-litter at the
service-station crossroads
alike instruct, distract.

The stone lip of a flower,
the lowest, on the left side,
on the government building.
stares through a different sun.

I lean on the warm stone
and sense its coldness.

The palaces of sense are
patchy after years of hopeless upkeep,
taxes, institutional requisitioning:
a public charge, largely.

A woman with her hair
fixed like a corpse's
is closed like a bank's vault against
even the Sanhedrin of the ranged
windows and towering blocks.

Yet, touched to pallor, she
knows day, abruptly,
as I, and the stone flower, abruptly,
suffer the cryptic change.
The turning-point of morning, and the
unmerging child,
like the sadness of the summer trees,
assert their changelessness
out of this day-change.

Light, the discovering light, is a beginning
where many stillnesses
yearn, those we had long thought long dead
or our mere selves.

In the moment of held breath
the light takes shape:

    now in Osiris, stepping
    along the reedy shore of sunset where
    stone skiffs manoeuvre through
    wild grass and the dark water-gates;
    now chipped among the textures of
    the chrome, the celanese, the rough-cast plaster,
    the stone flower, and my fingers resting on it;

In each at least light finds
one of its forms
and is:

even in the invisible neighbour,
periwigged, black, in hunting pinks,
or rinsing clouts beside the holy river,
who does not bother glancing up to see.

Not the Sweet Cicely of Gerardes Herball

(*i.e.*, ORIENTAL MYRRH, NOT ENGLISH MYRRH)

Myrrh, bitter myrrh, diagonal,
Divides my gardenless gardens
Incredibly as far as the eye reaches
In this falling terrain.
Low-curled in rams-horn thickets,
With hedge-solid purposefulness
It unscrolls, glistening,
Where else the stones are white,
Sky blue.
No beetles move. No birds pass over.
The stone house is cold.
The cement has crumbled from the steps.
The gardens here, or fields,
Are weedless, not from cultivation but from
Sour unfructifying November gutters,
From winds that bore no fennel seeds,
Finally, from a sun purifying, harsh, like
Sea-salt.
The stubbled grass, dragonfly-green,
Between the stones, was not so tended.
Mild animals with round unsmiling heads
Cropped unprotested, unprotesting
(After the rind of ice
Wore off the collarbones of shallow shelving rock)
And went their ways.

The bitter myrrh
Cannot revive a house abandoned.
Time has bleached out the final characters
Of a too-open Scripture.
Under the staring day
This rabbinical gloss rustles its
Leaves of living darkness.

With the maps lost, the voyages
Cancelled by legislation years ago,
This is become a territory without name.
No householder survives
To marvel on the threshold
Even when the evening myrrh raises
An aromatic incense for
Far ivory nostrils
Set in the vertical plane of ancient pride.

Civility a Bogey OR
Two Centuries of Canadian Cities

Chinashop at seaborde,
 a speckled chinashop
in the hard-wheat flat-land,
 a red-sand chinashop
  in pine-scrub:
and in between the granite cup dangled by the pump.

 Came big bull buildings,
  sharded and shoaled
 even the moustache-cup,
  held a board-meeting,
 stood, or sat smoking,
  cratered the moonlight.
Mouseholes rustled with paper
and by then Hallowe'en was a prance of reeking horses.

 Chinashops tame bulls
  in time,
 glass and enamel
annealed have the glitter
 of schist, or a gunmetal
  sheen. The ceilings
tilt, and the filled ground flounders.

 Earth, air, firewater
crack their joints, daring
  a dust-up;
no man can shape his own rump
though the seats of the mighty swing   sunlight.
        claw in the
        and crane

Where was bullshop, boardroom
        sky laps leisurely
round wrack and jetty.
        Pigeons chuckle at
plunging and all the fuss and feathers,
    and the docks of seaborde, flatland, pinescrub
shine through the windy night in their dark moorings.

                To walk the earth
                is to be immersed,
                slung by the feet
                in the universe:

The blessed heads learn smiling upside down
            shored on a crumb
whether in hinterland or town.
            It's all one.

Tennis

Service is joy, to see or swing. Allow
All tumult to subside. Then tensest winds
Buffet, brace, viol and sweeping bow.
Courts are for love and volley. No one minds
The cruel ellipse of service and return,
Dancing white galliardes at tape or net
Till point, on the wire's tip, or the long burn-
ing arc to nethercourt marks game and set.
Purpose apart, perched like an umpire, dozes,
Dreams golden balls whirring through indigo.
Clay blurs the whitewash but day still encloses
The albinos, bonded in their flick and flow.
Playing in musicked gravity, the pair
Score liquid Euclids in foolscaps of air.

Snow

Nobody stuffs the world in at your eyes.
The optic heart must venture: a jail-break
And re-creation. Sedges and wild rice
Chase rivery pewter. The astonished cinders quake
With rhizomes. All ways through the electric air
Trundle candy-bright disks; they are desolate
Toys if the soul's gates seal, and cannot bear,
Must shudder under, creation's unseen freight.
But soft, there is snow's legend: colour of mourning
Along the yellow Yangtze where the wheel
Spins an indifferent stasis that's death's warning.
Asters of tumbled quietness reveal
Their petals. Suffering this starry blur
The rest may ring your change, sad listener.

Unbroken Lineage

Pinfeathered Fancy from his high perch views
His broad domains, and rests a Royalist.
Though in the menial round he can subsist
Crafting for rats through the obscurest mews,
Or hop with twittering chickadees, enticed
By winter berries, or in the smokey blues
Of the October steppe mournfully cruise
Nightlong with the last tufted anarchist,
Yet from his pinnacle piercing all disguise
He will see marbled gardens, the young prince kissed
By imperial doom, kings eyeless, mad, resist-
ing toppling combers, or a King of the Jews.

Mews, meadows, steppes, bear still the fabled kings
Long after roofless courts are left to chalky whirring things.

Butterfly Bones OR
Sonnet Against Sonnets

The cyanide jar seals life, as sonnets move
Towards final stiffness. Cased in a white glare
These specimens stare for peering boys, to prove
Strange certainties. Plane, dogsled and safari
Assure continuing range. The sweep-net skill,
The patience, learning, leave all living stranger.
Insect – or poem – waits for the fix, the frill
Precision can effect, brilliant with danger.
What law and wonder the museum spectres
Bespeak is cryptic for the shivery wings,
The world cut-diamond-eyed, those eyes' reflectors,
Or herbal grass, sunned motes, fierce listening.
Might sheened and rigid trophies strike men blind
Like Adam's lexicon locked in the mind?

Jonathan, o Jonathan

The spokes of sun
have pronged and spun:
a bowling barrow – paddle-wheel – or rein
held taut. Careening
early this morning
shod hooves flaked the loose tiles. Sky opened. Horning
farness flooded through.
The high-swivelling blue,
the wet-clay cumulus, and the rough fleur-de-lys
fringing it, ensource
an unroofed universe,
lettuce-cool largeness. The wrenched miles swing and course,
rivers of speed.
The oven-bread
of earth smokes rainbows. Blind stars and swallows parade
the windy sky of streets
and cheering beats
down faintly, to leaves in sticks, insects in pleats
and pouches hidden
and micro-garden.
At the kitchen-door of their forwardfold backslidden
munching wishes, men,
shouting and toppling
smokestacks like Saturday children, suddenly crane
for the still Make-wish.
Where the roofs slope and flash
are hearts pungent and herbal for the sungold wheels to crush.

Meeting Together of
Poles and Latitudes (In Prospect)

Those who fling off, toss head,
taste the bitter morning, and have at it –
thresh, knead, dam, weld,
wave baton, force
marches through squirming bogs,
not from contempt, but
from thrust, unslakably thirsty,
amorous of every tower and twig, and
yet like railroad engines with
longings for their landscapes (pistons pounding)
rock fulminating through
wrecked love, unslakably loving –

Seldom encounter at the Judgment Seat
those who are flung off, sit
dazed awhile, gather concentration,
follow vapour-trails with shrivelling wonder,
pilfer, mow, play jongleur
with mathematic signs, or
tracing the forced marches make
peculiar cat's-cradles of telephone wire,
lap absently at sundown, love
as the stray dog on foreign hills
a bone-myth, atavistically,
needing more faith, and fewer miles, but
slumber-troubled by it,
wanting for death that
myth-clay, though
scratch-happy in these (foreign) brambly wilds;

But when they approach each other
the place is an astonishment:
runways shudder with little planes
practising folk-dance steps or
playing hornet,
sky makes its ample ruling
clear as a primary child's exercise-book
in somebody else's language,
and the rivers under the earth
foam without whiteness, domed down,
as they foam indifferently every
day and night (if you'd call that day and night)
not knowing how they wait, at the node, the
curious encounter.

The Fallen, Fallen World

When, breathing murk and apprehension of
Slow sure estrangement from the sun,
Night and the withering Arctic wind explore
The vacant corridors that are allowed
Us for our enforced passage,
We are, in snow and sleep's despite,
Straitly sustained.

REVOLUTIONARIES

Some that the sun in happier days burnished
Gather an odd intensity
As they had learned, ungalaxied, to centre
Fuel and fume, and in fair arrogance
To, unconsumed but self-consuming, burn,
Till see them! wayside smithies for the metals
Of a waste warlike time.

IDEALISTS

There are those who in moan and misery
Stray desolate along the steely river
Where in May's clarity the blond boy handled
Stones silvered for his dam, and o, repent
That under starlight, dissolute and lovely,
He to the angel's urgency gave way
And won a sunless summer for his soul
Which Jacob onetime spurned for morning's stone:
And among ice and yellow floes and dense
Sealed barren thorns and thickets, these lament,
And in their sinewed penance strive
To win belief in a new burgeoning.

And, some, alas, who from the summit see
The seasons' sure resolve, and having sounded
Dayspring in the Magnificat, and sensed
The three-day darkness on the eternal's doorstep
Not once, but more than once, now are but weary
Because the hope is certain, and the sound
And sense are for them qualities of time
Where meaning mocks itself in many echoes
Till it is meaningless;
They, stubborn, on the frozen mountain cling
Dreaming of some alternative to spring.

Yet where the junco flits the sun comes still
Remote and chilly, but as gold,
And all the mutinous in their dungeons stir,
And sense the tropics, and unwitting wait.
Since Lucifer, waiting is all
A rebel can. And slow the south returns.

Grammarian on a Lakefront Park Bench

Skewer my heart and I am less transfixed
than with this gill that sloughs and slumps
in a spent sea. Flyspecked and dim
my lighthouse signals when no ships could grind.
Sargassos of inheritance thrid through
choked day, swollen to almost total swamp.
Could I be pierced and spun,
pronged for a Midway,
that would be leaping.
     But not life.
White-teethed after their plates of kale, these smilers
stroll across triangles of blue, rectangles
of purple-blue, collages of green-blue
and shellack orange. All their newspaper sky
squints through the milky midday Sunday
to read them, carelessly,
confusing saddle-pears and sundecks.
The vintage elms wither by moral accident.

35

Atlantis and the Department Store

If I were a rebel would I find myself
At the March sounding of crows,
Dwelling a scurfy, hectic,
In filial piety frail, but ox-boned
Prince
East beyond Muscovy, cribbed in an endlessness
Smokey, reeking with damp,
Except one day, at crow-call,
Blaze of pure light in archetonics mounted
To the last circle
Of the fat saints, haloed in gold, millenniums
Lost in pale blue?

Indeed I did not hate
The tedious forenoon hallways,
Afghans, and carpets where the tiny table-legs
Pricked for depth and threads entangled them,
Tallow cold, stove heat,
Even the plain in luminous brown flood
And nets made ready for the weir.
Hate is unbearable but these I bear;
Knowing them all to despair, long since,
Washed me up over the knuckles of time
To the carpets in cinema foyers (red), and splendid
Echoing stairways behind soiled concrete walls
Forgotten by the emporium's hierarchies
Stunned on their steady escalators
Within.

The World Still Needs

Frivolity is out of season.
Yet, in this poetry, let it be admitted
The world still needs piano-tuners
And has fewer, and more of these
Grey fellows prone to liquor
On an unlikely Tuesday, gritty with wind,
When somewhere, behind windows,
A housewife stays for him until the
    Hour of the uneasy bridge-club cocktails
    And the office rush at the groceteria
    And the vesper-bell and lit-up buses passing
    And the supper trays along the hospital corridor,
Suffering from
Sore throat and dusty curtains.

Not all alone on the deserted boathouse
Or even on the prairie freight
(The engineer leaned out, watchful and blank
And had no Christmas worries
Mainly because it was the eve of April),
Is like the moment
When the piano in the concert-hall
Finds texture absolute, a single solitude
For those hundreds in rows, half out of overcoats,
Their eyes swimming with sleep.

From this communal cramp of understanding
Springs up suburbia, where every man would build
A clapboard in a well of Russian forest
With yard enough for a high clothesline strung
To a small balcony...
A woman whose eyes shine like evening's star
Takes in the freshblown linen
While sky a lonely wash of pink is still
reflected in brown mud
Where lettuces will grow, another spring.

Death

I ask you how can it be thought
That a little clay house
Could stop its door
And stuff its windows forevermore
With the wet and the wind and the wonderful grey
Blowing distracted in
Almost night
And trains leaving town
And nine-o'clock bells
And the foghorn blowing far away
And the ghastly spring wind blowing
Through thin branches and
Thin houses and
Thin ribs
In a quick sift of
Precious terrible coldness?

New Year's Poem

The Christmas twigs crispen and needles rattle
Along the windowledge.
    A solitary pearl
Shed from the necklace spilled at last week's party
Lies in the suety, snow-luminous plainness
Of morning, on the windowledge beside them.
And all the furniture that circled stately
And hospitable when these rooms were brimmed
With perfumes, furs, and black-and-silver
Crisscross of seasonal conversation, lapses
Into its previous largeness.
    I remember
Anne's rose-sweet gravity, and the stiff grave
Where cold so little can contain;
I mark the queer delightful skull and crossbones
Starlings and sparrows left, taking the crust,
And the long loop of winter wind
Smoothing its arc from dark Arcturus down
To the bricked corner of the drifted courtyard,
And the still windowledge.
    Gentle and just pleasure
It is, being human, to have won from space
This unchill, habitable interior
Which mirrors quietly the light
Of the snow, and the new year.

Banff

The skiers dwindle up out of the valley.
The deft wind skims the snow
and with a sudden shift of temper
snarls and snaps at the puffy twigs
   spilling their whiteness on the blue-white drifts
     in patterns pencil-blue.
The long pines lean into the sky. Chalk-blue
the blank sky stares. Anthracite hill
  is blazing white on Tunnel's further flank
and Cascade blazing keen into the sun,
and white spume curls, clenches the green-blue Bow,
  the milk-green, solid-sliding, weltered Bow...
Savage hauteur, accepting cyclic Time
as but the lidding of a frozen Eye....

Hiatus

The weedy light through the uncurtained glass
Finds foreign space where the piano was,
And mournful airs from the propped-open door
Follow forlorn shreds of excelsior.
Though the towel droops with sad significance
All else is gone; one last reviewing glance,
One last misplacing, finding of the key,
And the last steps echo, and fade, and die.
   Then wanderer, with a hundred things to see to,
Scores of decisions waiting on your veto,
Or worse, being made at random till you come
So weeks will pass before you feel at home,
Mover unmoved, how can you choose this hour
To prowl at large around a hardware store?
When you have purchased the superfluous wrench
You wander still, and watch the late sun drench
The fruit-stalls, pavements, shoppers, cars, as though
All were invisible and safe but you.
   But in your mind's ear now resounds the din
Of friends who've come to help you settle in,
And your thoughts fumble, as you start the car,
On whether somebody marked the barrel where the glasses are.

Public Address

You cough too much.
The curd in the esophagus
Is a brave burgeoning. But the roots iwis
Plummet your groin.
Cough not then. Bear you like a man
Or clean you like a fish.

From a Provincial

Bent postcards come from Interlaken
In August, the tired emperor of the year;
On evening tables
Midges survey their planes of brief discovery
At a half-run. In Milton's candle's light
They so employed themselves.
Some die before the light is out.
Between darkness and darkness
Every small valley shows a familiar compass
Until like all before
Still most unknown, it vanishes.
In Caesar's camp was order,
The locus of their lives for some centurions
Encircled by forests of sombre France.
When day and life draw the horizons
Part of the strangeness is
Knowing the landscape.

November 23

A childhood friend of my friend has died suddenly.
We are not old, any of us;
None of us will be young, again.
Is it respect for my friend's grief (the estranger:
   his folded napkin and his cup
   empty, wherever people
   have waited seriously together
   alone),
Or is it the persistence
Of harbour fog-horn, cars,
My neighbour muttering to herself,
Not bothering not to, when
Stillness glimmers beyond there – just beyond the senses –
That makes me sweat with vertigo
On this peculiar shelf
Of being?

To Professor X, Year Y

The square for civic receptions
Is jammed, static, black with people in topcoats
Although November
Is mean, and day grows late.

The newspapermen, who couldn't
Force their way home, after the council meeting
&c., move between windows and pressroom
In ugly humour. They do not know
What everybody is waiting for
At this hour
To stand massed and unmoving
When there should be – well – nothing to expect
Except the usual hubbub
Of city five o'clock.

Winter pigeons walk the cement ledges
Urbane, discriminating.

Down in the silent crowd few can see anything.
It is disgusting, this uniformity
Of stature.
If only someone climbed in pyramid
As circus families can...
Strictly, each knows
Downtown buildings block all view anyway
Except, to tease them,
Four narrow passages, and ah
One clear towards open water
(If "clear"
Suits with the prune and mottled plumes of
Madame night).
Nobody gapes skyward
Although the notion of
Commerce by air is utterly
familiar.

Many citizens at this hour
Are of course miles away, under
Rumpus-room lamps, dining-room chandeliers,
Or bound elsewhere.
One girl who waits in a lit drugstore doorway
North 48 blocks for the next bus
Carries a history, an ethics, a Russian grammar,
And a pair of gym shoes.

But the few thousand inexplicably here
Generate funny currents, zigzag
Across the leaden miles, and all suburbia
Suffers, uneasily.

You, historian, looking back at us,
Do you think I'm not trying to be helpful?
If I fabricated cause-and-effect
You'd listen? I've been dead too long for fancies.
Ignore us, hunched in these dark streets
If in a minute now the explosive
Meaning fails to disperse us and provide resonance
Appropriate to your chronicle.

But if you do, I have a hunch
You've missed a portent.
("Twenty of six." "Snow? – I wouldn't wonder.")

The Swimmer's Moment

For everyone
The swimmer's moment at the whirlpool comes,
But many at that moment will not say
"This is the whirlpool, then."
By their refusal they are saved
From the black pit, and also from contesting
The deadly rapids, and emerging in
The mysterious, and more ample, further waters.
And so their bland-blank faces turn and turn
Pale and forever on the rim of suction
They will not recognize.
Of those who dare the knowledge
Many are whirled into the ominous centre
That, gaping vertical, seals up
For them an eternal boon of privacy,
So that we turn away from their defeat
With a despair, not from their deaths, but for
Ourselves, who cannot penetrate their secret
Nor even guess at the anonymous breadth
Where one or two have won:
(The silver reaches of the estuary).

Unfinished After-Portrait OR
Stages of Mourning

A human, human presence
    startles the streets,
  the blacktop suburb roads,
the insurance company's mica-glinting sidewalks.
  Has death not capped that smile?
Night lines of surf ride in on seablack, curling.

    A deft-lumbering gait
like the fat man's fat fingers skiffing cards down
  sets a course still past bobbing heads,
    past summer dacrons, kiosks,
      easy – till the heart's deadset,
        stopped at a curb,
  only pursues losing, over and over.

    Mirrory twilight frames
the Valentine porch of natural day.

    Start-and-stop despairs of
      that royal moving,
    keeps trying other sleights
as rockets roar for the interlunar
      only to piffle out in
        the ocean's suds.

This trip and gamble cannot be
    the best, the looked-for.
But even hanging a coat at the doorway sometimes
    barricades, cages, crams.

Backyard whistling is
some stranger's evening
grey, clear, and thin,
    nobody to plunder
in the unHectored ruins of the west
        fire, fire.

    Abandon, again, fails
to find melodic sequences, flounders past
    the courtly deferrant –
and canny – in sunflicker, or
snowed in beyond the hemlock swamps with not even
    coal-oil, only dog-chewed candle-ends;
        still able, too,
to read the dim books that lie small in the palm.

How come at this, from the cherishing
        hot-house of breath,
the costliness of crimson winter carnations?

    Washed, ribbed-out hulk
sidling the comfortable wharves,
        looks plural upwards.
Storm-jolly bulk and buttress and topstone steady
    configure a blind crucial sky
        wind or no wind
            for good.
But salvage rigs and consultants
    probe for scant profit.
        Yes. And yet

even the wind blowing from summer, buffeting
        the soft-snow streets
    enlarges. There is a human
        presence.

Thaw

Sticky inside their winter suits
The Sunday children stare at pools
In pavement and black ice where roots
Of sky in moodier sky dissolve.

    An empty coach train runs along
    The thin and sooty river flats
    And stick and straw and random stones
    Steam faintly when its steam departs.

Lime-water and licorice light
Wander the tumbled streets. A few
Sparrows gather. A dog barks out
Under the dogless pale pale blue.

    Move your tongue along a slat
    Of a raspberry box from last year's crate.
    Smell a saucepantilt of water
    On the coal-ash in your grate.

Think how the Black Death made men dance,
And from the silt of centuries
The proof is now scraped bare that once
Troy fell and Pompey scorched and froze.

    A boy alone out in the court
    Whacks with his hockey-stick, and whacks
    In the wet, and the pigeons flutter, and rise,
    And settle back.

The Artist

Let never a small white cat, on a November street,
Swerve past him into briers of oblivion.
    The city has so many mews and mulleins
    By daylight, and geometries of shadow
    By night, and is at all times no regarder
    Of cats or their unrectilinear
               Pursuer.

Too often as it is the buildings lapse
And leave him stranded on a vast white pier
With the small ship out in the spanking sunlight
Huzza'd by gulls, busy with funnel-work,
The gangplank banging vertical,
And all the tumbling convex of the planet
His area of subsequent pursuit
Who is no Polynesian with a paddle.

He, at once Hansel and Gretel, dropping crumbs,
Applies himself to penetrate the forest
But to maintain a sensible base where bread
Is baked, and axes honed, and lumber loaded.
And always in the evening, in the glades
Deep beyond all his disciplines allowed for,
When the last bird has eaten the last crumb,
He falls in love with the old witch
Who lives wild day and night in her candy house,
And too late, having offered up his flesh,
Resents the cage where she will fatten it
For her more succulent feeding.
Her he incinerates, of course, at the eleventh hour,
Recalling his parental obligation
Towards the conniving woodcutter and his wife

(Who discount his reversing of their roles
Yet count on his return).

See him, plump-cheeked with recent misery
Loom on their clearing and
                               cancel their crime.
No wonder the woodcutter's wife,
Wanting her role back, and to get on with her work,
Frets the bloat phoenix, and finally forced
By ennui, plants catnip in her garden
   Knowing full well the white cat is the favour
      The poor fool fattened for
         And will not follow far.

Easter

Now that the eve of April brings
  A delicacy of light at the day's end
    The bulge of earth seems again comic, and,
      On it, the city sails along the swerve
      Into that depthless diapason, pink,
Absurd, queer as a chemist's liquid, cloudless,
  Then filmed, then wind-fomented
    And flashed and flung about with rivers of rain.

    After the blur of doves the milky air
    Lulls, and listens, and there
    Is the sorrow of all fullness.
But on the hillside the frail tremulo
  Of a new dayspring, eggshell and lilac, wanders
    Through the drenched quiet branches.

A bird sings, forceful, glorious as a pipeorgan,
And the huge bustling girth of the whole world
Turns in an everywhere of sunwardness
Among the cloudcarved sundering of its oceans.

Extra-Political

THE THORNED SPEAKS (WHILE DAY HORSES AFAR)

The sickness has passed from me
of thinking that the flinching leaves
are frozen of all motion because my eye
falls on them. Muteness bereaves

my all but looking.
And yet, in the autumnal stooking
on the upslope stonewalled field
deep in my days and feeling, I am healed:

not harking
lest the leaves smite me, their ways. Breaking
our mutual trance is not the vow
the shining knight, this large-breathed Day, will go

heralding, deeding for, and seeking out
in grassy place, by vigil stone.
We strangely pierced together twine – a plait
over his lonely lady's shoulder thrown.

Tree, I, all other tresses, caught
in the cloistering metal of her thought.
   She wakes, alone, for him, this
      mirrored dimness,
         as we for her
           are.

Intra-Political

AN EXERCISE IN POLITICAL ASTRONOMY

Who are we here?
boxed, bottled, barrelled
in rows?
Comestibles with the trick
of turning grocer, shoplifter
or warehouse trucker, or sometimes,
in faery-false springtime
the lion-hearted four-foot haggler
with a hot dime?

Games are too earnest.
These packaged us-es
are to the gamboling of real nourishment
as mudcake to transmuted sun.
Truth is, men chew and churn (in rows
or squares, or one by one
like a domino on a walled tennis court)
galactic courses:
chlorophyll, mutton, mineral salts
pinpoint multiple sunrise, and
cram us with incendiary force;
or we ingesting cede
the solar plexus its serenes of sky,
till every sunborn creature
may lume deepforest pools, and floodlight
his architects; find, too,
lenses for micro-astronomical
amaze (he – transport! –
SNEEZES).

Who plunges away
from the inexorable of
weaving orbits, like a colt
hurtled from his gentle pasturing
by a through freight?

(Space with its purple eye
marks his fixed field
and not his helter-skelter heels.)
Fixity of our sun-selves in our courses –
that willed harmonics – is
nothing we know to date,
nothing we know
who do know fearful things.

Look at that platinum moon,
the sky still muslin pale inspiring
doom-sweet violation.
But ask the lone balloonist.
Zones of ultramarine
clutch at his jugular,
and when he engineers his venture,
a Vandal, loving, he lays waste;
the fields and folds Horace could celebrate
strip back to rainsoak
and Rome still baldly suns in its
imperial distances.
(Nothing inert may, in stone, space, exist – except as
our clocking selves insert it.
We move too far from ways of weightlessness.)
Space is a hazard.

Yet this pre-creation density
presses: our darkness dreams of
this heavy mass, this moil, this self-
consuming endless squirm and squander, this
chaos, singling off
in a new Genesis.
(Would it perhaps set swinging
the little horn-gates to new life's
illumined labyrinths if, released
from stifling,
creatures like us were planet-bathed
in new-born Light?)
(Glee dogs our glumness so.)

Dreams, even doubted, drive us.
Our games and grocery-store designs

are nursery-earnest,
evidence.
Strait thinking set us down in rows
and rigged the till.
But being bought and eaten
is, experienced, enough
to change this circular exchange.
And cringing from such courses
compounds confusion:
a new numerical excess
of us-es.

We set up shop after,
poach as we might, nothing else much remained
but tufts of fur and insect skeletons?   *dear*
And energy hasn't minded
phoenixing for us in our nonce?

But even our own energy
will out. String beans
and coronal pyres of sleep
keg up. These city shelves,
this play emporium,
wobble on nitroglycerine.

If, with dainty stepping, we unbox ourselves
while still Explosion slumbers,
putting aside mudcakes,
the buying, selling, trucking, packaging
of mudcakes,
sun-stormed, daring to gambol,
might there not be an immense answering
of human skies?
a new expectant largeness?
Form has its flow,
a Heraclitus-river with no riverbank
we can play poise on now.

(George Herbert – and he makes it plain –
Guest at this same transfiguring board
    Did sit and eat.)

Watershed

The world doesn't crumble apart.
The general, and rewarding, illusion
Prevents it. You know what you know in your heart
But there is no traffic in that direction,
Only acres of stained quicksand,
     Stained by the sun
That lingers still at a Muscovite level, ignoring
The clocks in the wrists and the temples, and up in the towers
That you see as you walk, assuming the earth your floor
Though you know in your heart that the foot-hold really is gone.

(I saw you come out of the painted grove, my buck,
With the bruise of leaf-wet under your eyes,
     In a shy terrible blaze.
   The painted grove, hung stiffly with cold wax
   And fading pigments, issued you complete
And tissued then in myriad light-spots, swivelling
Into sheerest space. It was bright and spacious and neat
With everything moving, pricking from points of clear:
     Day-bourne.)

There is a change in the air:
The rain and the dark and the bare
Bunched trees, in pewter fresco, square
From the window. Yes, and you know
In your heart what chill winds blow.
And the clocks in the temples, in all the towers, sound on
(Quarter and half), and the gutters flow, and the sour
Rain pastes the leather-black streets with large pale leaves.

Mordent for a Melody

Horsepower crops Araby for pasture.
T.V. glides past the comet's fin.
No question, time is moving faster
And, maybe, space is curling in.

Seething with atoms, trifles show
The Milky Way in replica.
Clip but a fingernail, and lo!
A supernova drops away.

Spinning ourselves at stunning speed,
Within our envelope of air
We spin again. The derricks bleed
To spark us round and round our sphere.

Things are arranged in series. What
Appears but once we never see.
Yet someone, streaking by then, caught
Crescendos of conformity.

Reported them a unit, proved
Proliferation serves its turn.
(How can the Engineer above
Refuel, at the rate we burn?)

Sleep has a secret tempo. Man
Swerves back to it, out of the glare,
And finds that each recurring dawn
Wakes Rip Van Winkles everywhere.

Dance of the midges in the warm
Sand reaches of infinity,
May this invisible music swarm
Our spirits, make them hep, and we

Sing with our busy wings a gay
Pas de million until our singeing-day.

Apocalyptic?

"We must accept the baptism of the gutter"
(Yeats). "We must love one another or die"
(some other poet). "We must eat and marry
And give our children college educations,
Write fair insurance for our wives and die
If possible before retirement," say
The despised who despise in innocence.
Accept, yes. Choose what we accept. *And* die.
Create yes, even if genes
Are marbled through with radioactive rays
And promise a millennium of cripples
And fools of God (will they do better?). Praise
The light, that we can breathe it, and defy
All mustiness around the living I.
This treadmill turns by us, and of itself.
For just this sparrow time, we tramp in day,
Our one arc under the magnificent sky.
If love first turn the doggedness to dance
Then staggers on the why, still monuments
Hover oblique to a descending wheel.
Figures of fun before us and behind
Glimpse wry stone silhouettes, and find an eye
Emptily searching theirs. Old scores for hautboy
Sing from forgotten winters. The faint cry
Where the wheel verges upwards peals
A splendour in our hearts. An amnesty
No prince declared yet shines. The old man reels.
Love in absurdity rocks even just men down
And doom is luminous today.

Apocalyptics

By the door draught in the hut
Stevie snuffles. Streaks of smut
From the Quebec stove soil his chin.
He jerks when someone new comes in.
Snowpads melt around the door.
Skates have gouged the wooden floor
And wet has worked its fibres loose
Like corn-silk, grey. An old caboose
Serves any animal need like this.
Dazed by the cold the people twist
Their skate-straps tight, or thud their heels,
Their eyes as glittering-dumb as eels.
Prisoners of the cold endured
To get here, they are now absurd:
Lining the benches, chafing hands
At the stove apron, winking sands
Of sleep out of their glazy eyes.

While outside on the jewelled ice
The mongrel of God skitters and skids,
Frolicked in snow to his stiff eyelids.
He yaps and invites for all he's worth,
And hour by violet hour summer nibbles her way north.

II

Among the ringing lockers
The giggling girls are hid.
Chlorine smells, and sweat and tennis
Shoes and rubber caps. A venice
Sunlight streaks the sloppy tiles
And toilet-small compartments – miles –
Lead every way under a lid
Of sky accidian blue. The girls
Giggle and the turnstile whirls
On the streetside of this wall.
You smell exhaust from new-parked cars,
Fish and onions, and cigars
From the men's cabinets beyond
(A similar clashing locker sound
But guffaws instead of giggles)
And little Stevie has the wiggles.
Mother, strapping bosom in,
Fails to take the message in
Till he weeps and piddles there
In a sunshine of despair.
Nobody can thread the maze
Out of this pre-baptismal place.

On this empty sea outside
The bird of God waits and rides
The marcelled water, mercy stern,
While hours on hours steadily westward burn.

The city is a jungle jim.
Some of its bars and levels
And uprights
Are soap-soaked wood, some the
Sooty wires scallop-top fences for
Ruined gardens are made of.
The mats are used carpets, and
Rusty grass threaded with shepherd's purse.
And there are plastic portions,
Scaling iron,
And new paint bright on pole-new parts,
And steel of course. And steel.
Because a shepherd climbed after one sheep
Some climb here.
Because a fresco painter swung on scaffolding
Some swing.
Because of old agility on rigging
Some run along aux matelots.
All must still feed.

Physicists have broken through; some are dismayed to find
The new air they inhabit
They share with poets.
Governments (who?) can misconstrue
Use, though,
Make physics instrument of smarmy talk
On gravel level, in the late basketball sunlight.

And poets in potentia
Keep everyone
Busy on the jungle jim,
Either by wry example or the
Fomenting of frustration.

Rivers build up estuaries
To butt and foam at, dam themselves,
Excite old tensions between land and sea
(with vapours arbiter).

But these marvels, scrambling the crazy structures,
Each in his fashion,
Are not sediment,
Not instruments –
People, every one with a different world, from
Supernovae to amoeba in his soul,
Craving act, and harmony (shebang!).
Bewildered
Each broods in his own world
But half believes
Doctrines that promise to,
After some few suppressions here and there,
Orchestrate *for* all worlds;
But acts, meanwhile, if witlessly;
Cold-shoulders, really,
Those (who?) "suppressors"
(Or there'd be ding-dong now).

In Bowles Lunch, in the passage to
the washrooms and the alley exit,
They have an old piano, in case of
a wedding, or 30-years-medal party for one of the ones
who lope and sway and pick at things on any of the
Twenty-four (24) levels above.
Don't you suppose
Anything could start it?
                              Music and all?
                                        Some time?

Rich Boy's Birthday Through a Window

Some sod-cart dropped a weed.
Limp, dragging its roots and clotted dust
It lies in the high-altitude main street.

When the squaw and the pony farmer
Walk to the hardware store
Their shadows, smaller and in sharp focus
Seem brisk, alive with tensions
In pulled off-triangle shape.

The cars park in the queen's sun
Like inedible candy.

Upslope, below the treeline
The conifers fade to dry-moss colour,
Old snapshot-blue; below the rockwall
A long score in the mountain's flank
Shows where the open iron seams are worked
Even in tourist season.
The peaks saw-tooth the Alberta noon.

Things of the heart occur here.
Some wilt before sea-level.
Some are tamped down in the
Icelandic poppy beds
Under the cabin-walls.

Tip-alien, rigged like a court monkey
A bell-hop from the railroad chalet
Darts through the sun. And piercing, piercing,
A saxophone shrills on the
Ionic shore, at Marathon.

Our Working Day May Be Menaced

From this orange-pippery –
Where without violation
We force (the technique is of course secret)
The jumbled fruit to disgorge, severally,
Seed without juice,
Where parakeets are on the p.a. system
And all the walls are wattle
(Ehyoe hae-dee) –
   Madeleine, off the assembly line –
      which, in the glare and spindle of
      Hawaiian cottons, sea-light, mountain dust,
      and shoals and Takakaws* of oranges,
      is indeed form
      rather than fact –
         Since every cage is freighted
         With apron boys, coffee boys, the ladies
         Who feed and brush the evening shift of parakeets,
   Chooses the extension bridge
   (Windy at sunset)
   Rather than waiting for tiled egress, where the
   Cars debouche, below
   Weavy with green shadow and lamps burning.

...Madeleine's mamma knew.
Her foreman grudgingly, and we
With unrest, sensed, in her,
A certain clarity, a caritas,
But wood-wild....

A person has a nature.
I note hers only that I may bear witness.
Her silhouette high on the span
Focussed us then, for the quick –
Occurrence? A hard designation. It was

*Takakaw is a waterfall in the Canadian Rockies.

As if a spoke of the final sky
Snagged her suddenly.
For what seemed only one
Queer moment, she was swept
In some sidereal swerve,
Blotted sheer out of time; then spurned
Back to the pebbles of the path
(After the footbridge), where
Heartstain of sun
Still blurred the airfloor dark.

An evening delegation called, concluded
She is not schooled to cope.
                              It was our guess
She feels perhaps she nourishes a
Shameful little something of a bruise
In at the fusion-point of those peculiar
Burning-wires under the breastbone.
Some of us, privately piqued, privately speculate.

A calling from our calling?
In the œconomy of the clairvoyant,
Or some high-pillared parliament
We gave election, in an elated moment
Too rare for conscious purpose,
Can it have come to light that
The thirst for perfect fruit abroad
Has now been superseded, or subsumed
Under a new, more radical, craving?
Can they have appointed
A locus elsewhere for us?
Our mocha faces are too bland for trouble.
Yet may we, when the morning steam-cocks open
For our new day aloft
Find there is come about a universal

Swallowing-up
(Proceedings against Madeleine alone
Clearly being absurd)?
With only the racks and vats,
The lifts and cages left, uncrated and forgotten,
And the pipes steaming thinly
Under a fading crescent?

Stray Dog, Near Ecully

The dog called Sesamë slewed out
   Under the Norman arch, open
For the gardener's walked bicycle. No doubt
   On some wild leash still, in three-legged loping

He circles the grey stone and barley fringe
   Of the Roman amphitheatre, canting
To quit the guide, the stopped sun, the mélange
   Of Rome's new coin-conducted legions. Panting

He sloughs all touring finally, in the shade
   Of a wild apricot-tree, not glancing up.
Fire-points in his sad eyes fix on the fading
   Campagna ghost. A Rouault hoop

The limited landscape wobbles down
   Its sandy track of planetary time.
Back in the courtyard, through the hills around
   Deployed, they search, shouting, "Séy-sáhm, Séy-sáhm."

Identity

Half-sleeping, unbewildered, one accepts
The countless footsteps, the unsounding thud,
Not even asking in what company
One seeks the charnel houses of the blood.

Some mornings when the naked courtyard dwells
With listless sun, or when a darkening sigh
Stirs the old air along the quarried halls
One is aware of many passing by.

But on this sheet of beryl, this high sea,
Scalded by the white unremembering glaze,
No wisps disperse. This is the icy pole.
The presence here is single, worse than soul,
Pried loose forever out of nights and days
And birth and death
And all the covering wings.

So pressed, aloft, the errant angel sings.
Should any listen, he would stop his breath.

Rigor Viris

One bland ellipse in cornflower blue
Fans out beyond the gunnysack.
The profiles of Egyptian smiles
Confuse the clues these chimneystacks
Suggest of smoking miles,
    Wed smoke to sun instead,
    And blazon that parade
  Of all intolerables, in flowing frieze,
Against a pink brick wall in a dun autumn.

    Can this sere serried dance revive him now
      Whose imminent demise
      Stales the blown sky, and air
      Embattled, and lends glare
    To dying light in a lost season (how
      Ragged among the slag he sprawls
      Deployed within a static plan:
      Along the trillion prism walls
      Of diamond creeps the prisoned man)?

Evening is come too close now
For breath to come between.
Leaves blacken on a silver bough.
The ocean's sullen green
Sprouts in the cruel white of foam-flowers, whittled
      for vanishing.
      Now, Child Pandora, lift the lid again
      And let the clamouring mysteries be dumb
      In this clear twilight contour must contain
      Its source, and distances with contour come
    Opening peacock vistas that can no man entomb.

Rondeau Redoublé

Along the endless avenue stand poles.
Divorced from origin, their end's obscure.
There are doors lined up all along these walls.
Some open by the clock, and some immure

no sick child gazing out, but furniture
For dentists, typists, or those crooked halls
To empty lofts lost countrymen endure.
Along the endless avenue stand poles.

Under the negro sun the full tide rolls.
Crowds straggle gradually. There are fewer
By 3 P.M. (with these a pigeon strolls).
Divorced from origin, their end's obscure.

Dark brings the estuary, no vein pure
Enough to bleed freely. Horizon's holes
Fill slowly. Lights. Night's for the amateur.
There are doors lined up all along these walls.

Neons blaze lonelier. The foghorn bawls.
Taxis are knowledgeable now, and sure.
The wary one eyes EXIT. It appals.
(Some open by the clock and some immure
Along the endless avenue.)

Voluptuaries and Others

That Eureka of Archimedes out of his bath
Is the kind of story that kills what it conveys;
Yet the banality is right for that story, since it is not a communicable
    one
But just a particular instance of
The kind of lighting up of the terrain
That leaves aside the whole terrain, really,
But signalizes, and compels, an advance in it.
Such an advance through a be-it-what-it-may but
    take-it-not-quite-as-given locale:
Probably that is the core of being alive.
The speculation is not a concession
To limited imaginations. Neither is it
A constrained voiding of the quality of immanent death.
Such near values cannot be measured in values
Just because the measuring
Consists in that other kind of lighting up
That shows the terrain comprehended, as also its containing space,
And wipes out adjectives, and all shadows
    (or, perhaps, all but shadows).

The Russians made a movie of a dog's head
Kept alive by blood controlled by physics, chemistry, equipment,
    and
Russian women scientists in cotton gowns with writing tablets.
The heart lay on a slab midway in the apparatus
And went phluff, phluff.
Like the first kind of illumination, that successful experiment
Cannot be assessed either as conquest or as defeat.
But it is living, creating the chasm of creation,
Contriving to cast only man to brood in it, further.
History makes the spontaneous jubilation at such moments less and
    less likely though,
And that story about Archimedes does get into public school
    textbooks.

R.I.P.

The floor of heaven is really
Diamond congoleum.
It is a rather private place
(The Asians guessed it closest)
Where one or two
Play:
At joss-sticks by the wash-cotton
Curtains; or the domino board; or simply
The upright with too-loose keys
But on the whole a lovely tone,
Where the spidery shadow of
The lilac-tree wanders.
These one or two are never
Any particular one or two
But, simply,
The One or Two
Which it is
Sufficient exaltation
To be.

On the Death of France Darte Scott

UPON THE BIRTH OF TWIN SONS WHO LATER DIED

For the gemini, lost in the womb
Of the fair May mother lost in the snow
In the wintry wastes the ancient alone should know
There is vastly room
From the mortal dominions yielded;
But not where the fields are gilded
With buttercups and the children's sun.
The purple arc of the polar night
Inscribes horizon for them, where light
Would nightless glow, could the winter wane
Before that winter inspire the twain
With the frore May mother's mortal chill.
The seven-months' boys are borne to ride
A snow-melled limitless flood of morning's tide
Who should, by a greening hill,
Sleep warm and still.

The others, not strange yet, not forlorn,
Sundered in summer, only themselves can mourn.

Jael's Part

The mother of Sisera in late afternoon,
Bewildered by the stirless dust,
Cried out, leaning and peering from the window
For Sisera and his spoils.

Its ancient flood weltered with rich embroideries
Dark Kishon billowed to the bloodening sun.

Flotsam of that defeat,
Sisera, out of the Day of Judges, paced
The darkening vineyard, a new alien
In time. The thorny thicket of the vinestems,
Ravaged and leafless, blackened under night.
But the metallic green of the horizon
Stirred in his mind gentle and terrible dreams
Of morning-mists, and a valleyside
Purple with fruit; dreams he had never known
Till now, under the dense dead briary branches.

Sisera's brow, withering with the vision that
Outstripped the Day of Judges, Jael saw.
And to her the olives ripened
And the day hung heavy upon them
And every stone on the ground cast its sharp shadow.
And Jael envied Sisera's cheerless voice
When he came to her, and bade her pour him water.
Milk she brought, and butter
In a lordly dish.

And in her haze-white evening,
Sprawled like a glutton, Sisera

Lay on the tentfloor of Heber the Kenite
Pegged to the dust under the smothering tentskins
By Jael, blessed above women
The wife of Heber the Kenite.

And Sisera's mother stood and stared where the wheels
Of the leaderless warcar scored the leafbrown evening.

Span

The last of the old men of the house of Eli
Had many sons. Both the fat boys
Feasted on festival meats before the altars.
The bullock-sons
And those whose cheekbones yellowed with wine-sweat
Knew moister pleasures, under the temple gates.

    First, of the two fat boys,
    Their lips still glistered with repast,
    Eli was reft. He sounded desolate praises
    Far off, among the rocks and stars.

All these, and all their sons – sinews
Toughened, since Egypt, in the rocky pastures
And under the tentskins under the purple sky
East, out of Egypt –
All these would Death smite,
Cheating the house of Eli of chapless age, and the ephod.

    The bearded ones feel envy, with remorse,
    And sullied vistas dwindle.

A Conversation

"First comes the queer pocket of quiet," he said.
He had no particular listener
For few can listen, on Saturday afternoon,
And the whirr of the ventilators, and the din
Of cellar-lights under cement-walled skylights
And cigar-smoke, made listening too hard.
Yet: "Before the debacle," he said
"Comes the queer peace." And he heard
Not the din, but that.
   "Fish have a way of wavering through water.
They don't beat with their fins. What is their death
To me? I can't confront
A tree to really know it, and feel odd
To exchange glances with a squirrel,
And wish to keep my springs of life
Private from the Big Eye.
Well then. The fish has died. I'll not intrude there."
(Night over ocean after, and then day
Magnificently, as immaterial
As it is now, going on now out there,
To us....
And then the ivory slivers of the skeleton
Sidling and sifting, in a slope, through green
And blue-green down....)

"Is it a new thing to be still?" A stranger
Entered the friendly circuit of his unfocus
And: "I remember," he went on,
"How it was, many years ago, to wait,
Lonesome and happy, in the organloft
On a May evening, with the applegreen
And the robin song stirring with delicate largeness
The tall cathedral shadows, till your fingers
Rounded, the tips of your fingers, and you dared
Not move, as if a fresh sweet-flowing wound
Would open if you did, and let you lie

In lovely death there on the crimson steps
Under the long pale windows."
(And as if it had happened and were over
You felt a distinct, elegant compassion
To hear the children on their rollerskates
Out in the darkening street.)

"Elegant?" said the first man,
"Those little vertebrae down on the ocean-floor?"
(And smiled.) "But in the shallow water
Sea is a burning-glass to sun,
And to look down, at those unwinking starfish,
Your eyeballs could explode."

The waiter dabbed his mop-cloth at the blur
Of half-moon spill and ash among their elbows.

"I want the loud sun," said the man,
"Through jungle, and a big brass horn
To wet my lips on. See, my lips are swollen.
The sun does that. Thundering down in hundredweights
Swarmed on the sun that thundered down before it
And beats you down and makes you fight.
                    I want
A big brass horn to blow."
        "But the debacle..." said the stranger, rising with
        An unhappy, nervous smile.

The Mirrored Man

Lot put his wife out of his mind
Through respect for the mortal lot:
She having dared to yearn defined
All that to him was naught.

So now we flee the Garden
Of Eden, steadfastly.
And still in our flight are ardent
For lost eternity.

We always turn our heads away
When Canaan is at hand,
Knowing it mortal to enjoy
The Promise, not the Land.

Yet the Cimmerian meadows know the sword
Flaming and searching that picks out
The children for this earth, and hurls the curse
After us, through the void.
　So each of us conceals within himself
　A cell where one man stares into the glass
　And sees, now featureless the meadow mists,
　And now himself, a pistol at his temple,
　Gray, separate, wearily waiting.

We, comic creatures of our piebald day,
Either ignore this burden, nonchalantly
(Dragging a dull repudiated house
At heel, through all our trivial ramblings)
Or gravely set ourselves the rigorous task
Of fashioning the key that fits that cell
(As if it hid the timeless Garden).
　I interviewed one gentleman so engaged,
　And he looked up and said:
　"Despair is a denial and a sin
　But to deny despair, intolerable."
The next week, so I heard, he used his key,

Walked over to the mirror, forced the hand
Of the young man, and left him
Drooping, the idle door of an idle cell
Mirrored at last. Such men are left possessed
Of ready access to no further incident.

One man unlocked his cell
    To use it as a love-nest.
By fond report, the mirror there is crammed
    With monkey faces, ruby ear-rings, branches
Of purple grapes, and ornamental feathers.
    Whatever winter ravages his gardens
No banging shutters desolate his guests
    Who entertain illusion as he wills it,
And grant him the inviolate privacy
    His hospitable favour purchases.

All of us, flung in one
Murky parabola,
Seek out some pivot for significance,
Leery of comets' tails, mask-merry,
Wondering at the centre
Who will gain access, search the citadel
To its last, secret door?
And what face will the violator find
When he confronts the glass?

Birth Day

Saturday I ran to Mitilene.

Bushes and grass along the glass-still way
Were all dabbled with rain
And the road reeled with shattered skies.

Towards noon an inky, petulant wind
Ravelled the pools, and rinsed the black grass round them.

Gulls were up in the late afternoon
And the air gleamed and billowed
And broadcast flung astringent spray
                    All swordy-silver.
I saw the hills lie brown and vast and passive.

The men of Mitilene waited restive
Until the yellow melt of sun.
I shouted out my news as I sped towards them
That all, rejoicing, could go down to dark.

All nests, with all moist downy young
Blinking and gulping daylight; and all lambs
Four-braced in straw, shivering and mild;
And the first blood-root up from the ravaged beaches
Of the old equinox; and frangible robins' blue
Teethed right around to sun:
These first we loudly hymned;
And then
The hour of genesis
When first the moody firmament
Swam out of Arctic chaos,
Orbed solidly as the huge frame for this
Cramped little swaddled creature's coming forth
To slowly, foolishly, marvellously

Discover a unique estate, held wrapt
Away from all men else, which to embrace
Our world would have to stretch and swell with strangeness.

This made us smile, and laugh at last. There was
Rejoicing all night long in Mitilene.

A Friend's Friend

This fellow is bewildered,
Puckers his eyes like querulous age
at a curb. His nails are bitten.
His still-young skin has the look of
thumbsmears on a hard-boiled egg,
half-shell, half wrinkled membrane
tougher to break.
As if the natal stars shortened his stirrups
and set his rocking-horse facing the west
he seemed ambitious.
Did some cynical gaffer
hand him the pan and sieve, talk of the canyon
where you squat in a mulch of pebbles
in the sun-eyed mountain's evening,
as if in the tilt of a page someone sick of the glare
reads easier so?
Somehow he has kept these tools in balance.
The presence of his angel burning him
to this bewilderment makes popcorn of the experience
he thought his life; he is munched now,
trivial snack, a movie interlude.
Gratuities will buy his beer
till all the jobs are boarded up against him
but he won't mind. He is by now
no longer kernel-proud;
Proof against mountain-sickness;
Well-nigh illegible.
A tinker likes hard times.

Far Off from University

The counter-confessional priest
at daybreak through limp whites
showed the sharp scapulae,
turned from his greased grill to take cash
and at the doorway, with his spatula
pointed, past sheds and fluted morning pigeons,
across the shining steel of crisscross tracks, to
the villainous hovel still sodden in night,
in spite of wire-thrum and the sky's empty clamshell.

Night-damp and cinder mash
draggled the rasp-grass round a
smouldering derelict caboose.

With faintly clashing gear the yards
bestirred themselves, for the forced marches
of the new day, in aluminium distance
or around corners – somewhere out of sight.

The fragrance of cool tar,
smoked coffee, wet
machine parts, seagulls, dawn,
jolted a hobo torpor. After the sour
senility of night, suddenly,
a more than animal joy, a sanity
of holy appetite awoke;
breast bared for its blind suckling
a more than mother leaned, drew breath, tendering.
Cement and weeds, sky, all-night diner, flesh,
gathered as being; fumbling, fed.

September Street

Harvest apples lack tartness.
The youngest child stares at the brick school-wall.
After the surprising *coup* at a late luncheon meeting
    the young man shifting for green concludes
the future makes his bitten thumb the fake.
    A convalescent steps around
wet leaves, resolving on the post-box corner.
    Next time, the young man glimpses,
he will be one of three, not the lone fourth
    susceptible to elation.
    Yellow. The pride saddens him.
A van grinds past. Somebody with
considerable dash and a strong left hand
plays "Annie Laurie" on an untuned piano.
    Granada will not rhyme with Canada.
The home-grown wines have sharpness.
    A scissor-grinder used to come
    about the hour the school let out
    and children knocked down chestnuts.
      On the yellow porch
one sits, not reading headlines; the old eyes
    read far out into the mild
        air, runes.
See. There: a stray sea-gull.

The Agnes Cleves Papers

Why did you come so young
Wearing a cool print-silk, when your arms are round
And your cheek lovely? Why did you meet me here
Where the evening past those muted curtains blows
In liquid verdigris and pearl,
And inside, all the orchestra has played
Is waltz and wedding dance and windy harbours
And the sweets of sophisticated shepherds
Or those in coonskin, leopard skin,
In discus-throwers' oil and olive sun?

What story do you want?
Tales of young love, or of that horse with wings
The pink-striped circus lady rode, standing?
Why should I tell such things
Except to force myself, your peer,
In the strange perfumed anterooms
Of the fastidious voluptuaries.
Have you remarked
How few persist in penetrating farther
And all the rumour that subsides after them
Is of some outdoor chill, some stony wonder
With monkey-puzzle trees sprouted from paving stones
   And mourning doves over the high wall
      And pomegranate seed spilled in the
         Cleft where sand and winter sun
           Drift to make small regular shadows?

I knew a Finnish student long ago
Who could not come out of a barbershop
And all that glass, without the look
Of a conspirator briefed for furtive action.
His hour was always early morning,
His locus factory gates, and air about him
Was butcher-paper, mottled and saturated,
And an offence to many.
Yet I remember how I envied him

On my first trip, with my thin documents
And no invisible dossier, nothing but a
Statistical identity.

    Go home my dear. It is too late
    And you are all abrim and pent
    And the dark streets are tilted to a vacuum
    Where things may happen.

Dour winter scatters salt on the windowledge
And smothers day in twilight, and at Tours
The tower is murmurous with eerie
Barbarian snow; and when the factory sounds
8 o'clock, from my room in the back of the house
I hear black water churning
Out where the street was,
And sense the lumbering passage of
The old black-iron tug in the lost canal
Under a weight of
Smoke, and oil smudge, and snow.
    Stories of Uncle Remus and the carrot-tops
Are used in the unusual after-breakfast
Lamplight to distract the children,
And, when these flag,
Accounts of Uncle, who went to Australasia
And in the far fantailed meridian
Of the Down Under may be this very moment
Riding the surf. Daydreams
Of foam and aquamarine and ochre sun
Disc woodenly about the windowplaces
Where the grey furry flakes feel at the panes
And sidle and sift and mound.
And the pale mother yearns for
A rocking chair and her childhood by the stove
    The day the postman failed to come
        And chickens froze on the roosts.

Alec drove a two-door sedan
And worked for the Continental Can;
When you looked at him you knew that he knew

How the blood of a gamebird spilled in snow;
Alone out there on a prairie mound
With a grain-tinged skyline narrowed around.

But Valerius in December could
Simply sit by the fire and brood
And you saw the skywheels turn and follow.
The plum-dark velvets were streaked with tallow
And the morning shine made foreheads grim
And the sword-sounds all were pewter and dim....
Then he would change when the people came
And though sleet fizzed outside, and inside flame
On the logs, he somehow made you see
A thundery midday in July
With all the long lawns violet green
And every wall showing a leaden sheen
And the stillness dancing in violet sparks
Where the tram careened down the empty tracks
Towards the lake-beach and the broad sand
That was bluebrown waiting and warm to the hand....
Valerius' mother died last year
And he's gone to Mexico, I hear.

They should have cardgames in the stations:
    Those flag-stops, with a crow or two
Slanting about, and a cedar row
    Half-dead and silted up with cinders,
And the trainman's car, missing two fenders
    And torn in the leather and stuffing half through.
For the soul's voice you need the crow,
    But for a man a game of cards
While the planets seed down their big backyards
    And the lonely acres ache all round
And apart from the wind there isn't a sound
    And the Quebec stove stales the air
Till the eyes stop seeing and simply stare.

Do you remember the vestibule
In rainy September, at 5 in the afternoon?
Sometimes I feel I have eternally
Been removing my rubbers there, my feather draggled

A little, in the short distance up the walk
From the overheated taxicab. My thoughts
Are fuzzy and whitish in previous awareness
Of the next hour. I can smell the coffee and hear
China, and ladies' voices, and the sound
Of tires on the wet street.
And I am taking off my rubbers.

In that circular apartment
There are too many doors.
One, for example, gives on a back-kitchen
Although there is no kitchen, and the half-light
Through green glass, and the dust on the preserving jars
And the outdoor chill and smell of paraffin
Are for some reason distressing.
God knows the hall outside is narrow enough
Though the stairs are worse.
Why is it necessary for me to have
So many means of egress?
The woven door in particular bothers me
With all its tall fawn dapper birds, and cobblestones,
And I would be less aware of the black draughts
If it were not there. And the doubledoor in the arc
Behind the daybed should open on
Grass, where the divinity candidates
Could talk, quietly, even by floodlight if need be.
Yet these too give on the hall, where it is scarcely possible
To see one's way, and any hour of the evening
A woman in a bathrobe bearing enamel ewers
Is always just about to disappear.
Tell me, would they object if I stopped up
Some of these doors?

In March you can see the geese from the highroad.
They are very white. The rim of the pond is muddy
And the keen blue of the sky and these voyaging clouds
Show from the round water
And a beat like echoes makes your eyelids flutter.
A red and white collie fusses around the geese
And it would be clumsy walking (after climbing
The new wire fence) to go down there

And why should courage be hailing you to go
Because it is muddy and March and there are a few
Sinewy snowy geese
          Stretching their necks?
The weed that moves here
Its lastyear's withered tassel, under the fencepost,
Will move and move like a silly thing all night.
It is alive. But the wind makes it so.
   Stone is a stranger fellow.
Little David had only his stones and a slingshot
Against the giant with the purple beard;
And the onlookers drank stonepure melted snow
And munched their grey beards, there on the chalky ridges.

   The old are sometimes savage, brutalized
   By scope and newness.
   And I am much alone, as well as old,
   And fearful sometimes of the tedious fondness
   Peculiar to my kind, where the soft light
   Plays among things remembered, and today,
   Since lighted of itself, must then be subjugated
   To venom and timidity.

   One evening, just a year or two ago,
   The simple penetrating force of love
   Redeemed me, for the last perhaps. I've seldom dared, since,
   To approach that; not that it would go out,
   But it might prove as centre of all
   Revolutions, and, defined,
   Limn with false human clarity
   A solar system with its verge
   Lost, perhaps, but illumined in
   A mathematical certainty
   And for my secret I would have a universe.
   The need to tell you is exciting
   And very bleak.

There ought to be a word cognate with love
For situations people find themselves
As means of coming into their

Foreknown specific gravity.
    No, it's of someone else I'm thinking now.
This plot is not among the magic stories
Although it has their dream finality.

But story-tellers when they singled out
Their characters, found them enhanced
By seablue, or a china nutmeg dayyard.
How is it that by now
The shaft of vision falling on obscurity
Illumines nothing, yet discovers
The ways of the obscure?...

Miss Rothsey, while her parents were alive,
Was an attentive girl, a little acid
Perhaps, and with odd taste in shoes.
Many who might have overlooked her otherwise
Paused afterwards to speculate
Where she came by her clothes –
They seemed an inconceivable cross-breed
By old Assyria out of Peter Pan;

She must have been in her late twenties
When she moved up to Canada.
Perhaps once she had burned her bridges
She wondered why it had seemed sufficient reason
That her brother and his wife offered to share
Their home. For that, they'd seldom seen each other
For twelve or thirteen years. And the strange city
Chilled her. She had once played in
The violin section of the
Cincinnati orchestra,
But now made little effort to discover
Strangers with musical interests
And quickly felt that she had lost her skill.

    It is banal to draw conclusions
    From the garish colours of the poisonous fungi.
    Even in terms like "deadly nightshade"
    The pallid horror is misleading.
    Poison itself should properly not be thought of

As an inherent quality. There may be
A range of harmonizing chemistry
Where arsenic would be balm and dandelion
And radish sinister and noxious to
Whoever brighteyed may frequent those lit
Elysian hillsides.

Garnet was a commercial artist.
First an artist. Charcoal drawn himself
    And by nineteen capable of
Enjoying tea with lemon under
A kitchen wall, in the spent sun,
Simply because he liked it.
His sisters taught him early to
Capture, capitulate to, privacy,
Without themselves knowing or meaning anything.
Under all their family association
Ran an assumed affection
Sweet, murmurous, halfheard under the ice
Of their accepted obligation to
    Be something,
        Be somebody
            (or, in one case, be anybody, in
                distinction, indistinguishable).
Garnet failed as an artist –
He was the first to cede this little earth –
Because he almost liked commercial art
At times: liked geometric pastel disciplines
And casual make-up conferences; preferred
Not to despise.
It was years later that I knew him first
(Perhaps that adolescence is
My gift to him).

Certainly when he hired as shipping clerk
In the export-import firm where, for ten years
Miss Rothsey had been in a
Meagre, secure administrative position,
At that time he had promise,
Not as an artist, but as businessman.
His limp striped shirts, and readiness

To ease a crisis, with a printer's apron on,
Hardly endeared him to the freight-shed boys
And did him damage in prestige.
But anybody's hint might have solved that.
He was not disenchanted with the arts
But since his marriage, with two boys at school now,
Wanted more money.
His wife? I met her at the office Christmas –
A sombre, nervous woman, older than Garnet
I'd judge, and absolutely without interest
In us, or registering as Garnet's wife.
A lot of that can simply mean
She didn't want to drink.
Yet it made sense of the long evening hours
Garnet would willingly tackle
If he could have the full lights burning
And joke with the night watchman.
And nobody considered
His working more and more under Miss Rothsey
Was anything his family would have minded.

    Do you remember, in the long gallery
    At the Museum, the big Egyptian frieze?
    What knowledge of the stars or of blood bondage
    Or the arithmetic of sacred polity
    Delineated morning by the Nile
    For the oxdriver or the riverboy?

Garnet made me feel tears, that way.
Certainly he would not have lived
The pious pattern out, husband and father
With neither kin nor keening until death.
Certainly Miss Rothsey never knew
About the tea and lemon, never mentioned
The Cincinnati concert hall,
And neither thought of these things. They cut down
Each other's stature, over affairs of invoices
And policies for the directors' meetings
And at times hated one another.
Yet that is what I meant. Because they met

Each could achieve a doomed specific gravity
And Antony and Cleopatra figured
Ruin in large, but set the style they held.

   Down on the levee army boys
   Are making breaches in the month of March
   To let the January rains pour into
   The detour roads and the lamented valleys
   And spare all pavingspace
   Leaving to rust the lace grill fronts
   Of oldfrance New Orleans
   And sparing cracked cement
   And urban privacy.
   The Sewanee River:
   Magnolia trees and sawdust yards
   And wicker chairs rocking in beaten doorways
   With coffee spice and sugar cane
   And denims on a line
   And the tin washtub left in cinnamon tree-shade
   And mongrels thin at ramble and the sound
   Of bloodwarm riverflow under the mudbanks:
   These are the country seen
   Under the culvert, when the sun breaks through
   For a short glorious spate.

Rust-coloured chintz, and Taylor-Statton attitudes
Could dominate a foreign policy
Were there no ghostly impetus, no knowledge
How the sea heaved up Iceland out of darkness,
Bleak, and the Altsheim of the elder sun
But thinly peopled.

The long years' march deadens ardour, a little;
Like nine-year-olds we eye clay figurines
That weep at supper on a storm-scoured beach
Under a peacock arc, and could be globed
In glass, and show our faces watergreyed
By diningroom window sunlight, in the safe
Odour of floorwax.

What I saw was an exhibition rocket.
Outside ourselves, time could be purpled so
In one swift trail over the inky grandstand.
The minutes, and the pebbles, and the dream
By daylight snowflakes muffled under pinbone,
Ghastly and very gentle, and the child's knees
Impatient, while he straps on rollerskates,
Are what I found like love, in case
I should see rocket only in my time.

Telling it in plain words
Makes me see how I feared the wrong thing.
The other centre, the known enigma –
All eyes I do not own, contours
That force familiarity where I would
Tumult and spurn like Pan – were the mountain passes
Pure out of thought; this iris bed
Is scarfed in dreadful mist
    And no sun comes
        Beyond the yellow stoneway....

(Set the pasture bar and close the gate.
The firelight and the cool piano keys
And the silktasselled curtain weight,
And the Shanghai-American marquis
And tires and tiredness, and the dingy freight
Toiling upevening into China tea
Are not distractions. They are the arena.
The scarlet satin tights are your colour
And from the cigargrapebloom of the stands
Radiate black wires down to the floodlit mat
Where the microphone dangles over – any one of them
If you prefer to chew a cigar this round.

    How wrong you are to think your glancing back
    Into the zones and corridors will long be tolerated
    Or, for that matter, looking will lead you back
    To the hill and the hoof-pocked dark between
    Eveningstar and mushroom.

The wild smell is the other side
Of the impenetrable world of stone
And is no athlete's incense.
After the match is called, before midnight,
We will go dreaming into secondhand junkstores,
Or go for a late sail out beyond the gap
And in the morning, you will see,
The children will be chalking hopscotch on
The Moscow streets, on Lima's cathedral square
Past beaky statue-shadows. . . .)

The Dumbfounding

Old . . . Young. . . .

The antlers of the ancient
members of the orchard lie
bleaching where the young grass
shines, breathing light;

the candles are carried
to seek out those in the cellars
granular in their lees:

because cobwebs are forked away
and the wind rises
and from the new pastures long after longstemmed sunset,
even this springtime, the last
   light is mahogany-rich,
      a "furnishing."

The Two Selves

All the cages are empty
and crusted dry.
Why do they hang from
your lintel and ceiling?

> The birds in the sky
> left this to me.

But your room is bare
as a customs shed,
and the cages at head-
level swivel, and there
is no *escritoire*....

> No, only a linen sky
> and a bicycle-tree
> somewhere, for me.

Your Philip Sparrow
scribbles his tracks
in the waterfront soot at
a warehouse door.

> That one? Maybe –
> there were many
> who flickered away.

And you *wait* for them here?

> Oh no. It is more
> like knowing the sound of the sea when you
> live under the sea.

Two Mayday Selves

The grackle shining in long grass
this first day of green casts
an orchid-mile of shadow
into the sun-meld, that marvel, those
meadows of peace (between the bird
and the curved curb
of the city-centre clover-leaf).

The aloof
tiers of offices, apartments, hotels,
schools, park branches, opal
heaven-hidden stars, the other
beholder – out there, here,
insect-sing, a cappella,
the sticky welter –
brilliance, buds,

June bugs –
steam into globules
on the hill domed over the moles'
palaces. Knuckled winter
and its grease-stiff hood: where
is it still? is it past
any convulsive gulp, any least
whistling whisker-work
on the lush park
green, on the princely
bird and his glossiness
(reminiscent of flies) and the rice-
perfuming light sifting
between that pointing distance
and this?

"Old ghoul, leather-tough diaphragm,
listen! – I am
holding *my* breath.
The power of the blue and gold breadth

of day is poured out, flooding, all
over all.
Come out. Crawl out of it. Feel
it. You,
too."

Pace

"Plump raindrops in these
faintly clicking groves,
the pedestrians' place, July's
violet and albumen
close?"

"No. No. It is perhaps the conversational side-effect
among the pigeons; behold
the path-dust is nutmeg powdered and
bird-foot embroidered."

    The silk-fringed hideaway
    permits the beechnut-cracking
    squirrels to plumply
    pick and click and
    not listen.

Pedestrians linger
striped stippled sunfloating
  at the rim of the
    thin-wearing groves

letting the ear experience this
discrete, delicate
clicking.

Twilight

Three minutes ago it was almost dark.
Now all the darkness is in the
leaves (there are no more
low garage roofs, etc.).

But the sky itself has become mauve.
Yet it is raining.
The trees rustle and tap with rain.
. . . Yet the sun is gone.
It would even be gone from the mountaintops
if there were mountains.

In cities this mauve sky
may be of man.

The taps listen, in the unlighted bathroom.

Perfume of light.

It is gone. It is all over:
until the hills close to behind
the ultimate straggler, it will
never
be so again.

The insect of thought retracts its claws;
it wilts.

Black-White Under Green:
May 18, 1965

This day of the leafing-out
speaks with blue power –
among the buttery grassblades
white, tiny-spraying spokes on the end of a weed-stem
and in the formal beds, tulips
and invisible birds inaudibly hallooing,
enormous, their beaks out wide, throats bulging, aflutter,
eyes weeping with speed
where the ultraviolets play and the scythe of the jets
flashes, carrying
the mind-wounded heartpale person, still a boy, a pianist, dying
    not
of the mind's wounds (as they read the x-rays) but
dying, fibres separated, parents ruddy and
American, strong, sheathed in the cold of
years of his differentness, clustered by two at
the nether arc of his flight.

This day of the leafing-out is one to remember
   how the ice crackled among
      stiff twigs. Glittering strongly
         the old trees sagged. Boughs
   abruptly unsocketed. Dry, orange gashes
the dawn's fine snowing discovered and powdered over.

...to remember the leaves ripped loose
the thudding of the dark sky-beams
and the pillared plunging sea
shelterless. Down the centuries
a flinching speck
   in the white fury found of itself – and another –
the rich blood spilling, mother to child, threading
the perilous combers, marbling
the surges, flung
out, and ten-fingered, feeling for
the lollop, the fine-wired

music, dying skyhigh
still between carpets and the
cabin-pressuring windows
on the day of the leafing.
Faces fanned by
rubberized, cool air
are opened; eyes wisely
smile.
The tulips, weeds, new leaves
neither smile nor are scorning to smile nor uncertain,
dwelling in light.
A flick of ice, fire, flood,
far off from
the day of the leafing-out I knew
when knee-wagon small, or from my
father's once at a horse-tail silk-shiny
fence-corner or this
day when the runways wait
white in the sun, and a new leaf is
metal, torn out of that blue
afloat in the dayshine.

Micro-Metro

I

Barber's; "Guitar Lessons"; used
raincoats on outdoor racks,
a many-money-place (closed
for refacing with glass bricks);

ivy-towelled, lonely-sunned,
lawn-folded, hedge-hid
homes; and unaproned
grease-dapper road-grid

all wires, lights, din;
square rooms with square holes
over stores; tea and mutton
smells of our kind: our walls

fall away, recoil
or pile up, a-gape
when the park greens unfurl –
grass rug, *tree* drape,

fountain (drinking), fountain (playing),
foot-paths, benches,
band-stand (but no playing),
a popsicle booth, wrought-iron fences.

11

Under the sun's spots
bandsmen rove
(peach satin, white spats)
littering the grave

slopes with parade-
silks, match-papers, plumes.
The colours are stirred by route-
rallying drums.

They are told what to play
and are dressed, almost ready
to line out the way:
people...walls...city.

Riding and Waves

Maybe not any longer
should the meek lover
at slack rein amble through the afternoon
snow-whinged, or sunflower-randy
with a black heart of seeds to take
mumbling home at the
cellardoor of day
past fading rooster-crates, past
CEMENT suddenly.

(why not cement?)

In Time

Stumps in the skull
feel smooth.
No juice. No punkwood.
Sheaves
of tall timber
sprout awkwardly – poplar clumps
        by the railway cut –
in a matter of years.

That's growth.

Smell the leaf-acid
in the new sky.

Until Silenced: To I.A.

(A PAKISTANI SCHOLAR, WHO QUOTED AND INTERPRETED
SOME LINES OF RUMI'S POETRY FOR ME
IN THE AFTERNOON OF FEBRUARY 15, 1965)

Persian lover, long dead, out of the night-
blackness, slick-roiling whirlpools, loving and
trembling and being changed,

    your lustre finds its foil
    in these by beach-fires, or miles
    inland who may learn of
    perilous waters but stand
    solid, so you are unreal:

after six hundred years, here,
a thousand miles from ocean
with the moon-rock bald in daylight
and the wind, searching, the
purifier, at loose,

    this winter sun glisters on
    washed cottons, amid a branch-tangle
    and morning quiet.

Thin wine of joy
threads your black-iris and this
resilient beeswax-coloured tendril.
Real. Real.

    The mourners about the streets
    pause, almost seeing suddenly
    clear evening, and a rose.

The Mourner

"Because the windows were boarded up
on us, though when the wind
blew in this dry tree-scaly scruff
or the swimmer's morning freshness, we can, now,
not securely remember,
but because the windows were
boards, one pencil beam
no longer diffused, no longer confusable
with the virtues of visibility,
but purely, narrowly,
compellingly
itself, is evidence that there is
Tree. Morning. Freshness. Even though
the windows have been boarded
up on
us,"
told the Mourner, moving
down the grass-blowing years, making
a day.

Many As Two

"Where there is the green thing
life springs clean."
    Yes. There is blessed life, in
    bywaters; and in pondslime
    but not for your drinking.
"Where the heart's room
deepens, and the thrum
of the touched heartstrings reverberates – *vroom* –
there I am home."
    Yes. And the flesh's doom
    is – a finally welcome going out on a limb?
    or a terror you who love dare not name?
    (No thing abiding.)
No sign, no magic, no roadmap, no
pre-tested foothold. "Only that you know
there is the way, plain,
and the home-going."

Outside the heartbreak home I know, I can own
no other.
    "The brokenness. I know.
    Alone."
(Go with us, then?)

July Man

Old, rain-wrinkled, time-soiled, city-wise, morning man
whose weeping is for the dust of the elm-flowers
and the hurting motes of time,
rotted with rotting grape,
sweet with the fumes,
puzzled for good by fermented potato-
peel out of the vat of the times,
turned out and left
in this grass-patch, this city-gardener's place
under the buzzing populace's
square shadows, and the green shadows
of elm and gingko and lime
(planted for Sunday strollers and summer evening
families, and for those
bird-cranks with bread-crumbs
and crumpled umbrellas who come
while the dew is wet on the park, and beauty
is fan-tailed, grey and dove grey, aslant, folding in
from the white fury of day).

In the sound of the fountain
you rest, at the cinder-rim, on your bench.

The rushing river of cars
makes you a stillness, a pivot, a heart-stopping
blurt, in the sorrow
of the last rubbydub swig, the searing, and
stone-jar solitude lost, and yet,
and still – wonder (for good now) and
trembling:

   The too much none of us knows
   is weight, sudden sunlight, falling
   on your hands and arms, in your lap,
   all, all, in time.

Words

Heraldry is breath-clouded brass,
blood-rusted silks, gold-pricked even threadbare
memorials of honour
worn,
a shield when napalm and germ-caps and fission are
eyeless towards colour, bars, quarterings.

A herald blares in a daybreaking
glory, or foolishly carols –
robin under a green sky – or, a
green earth-breaking tip, is still
but with bodily stillness, not the
enemy's voicelessness.

The ancient, the new,
confused in speech,
breathe on, involving
heart-warmed lungs, the reflexes
of uvula, shaping tongue, teeth, lips,
ink, eyes, and de-
ciphering heart.

Ps. 19

Clean is the word with *fear*.
Fear is to love high
and know longing for clear
sunlight, to the last ribcorner
and capillary – and wonder
if, so known, a sighing-
over-the-marshlands me
might all evaporate, wisp away.
Yet to love high
is with this very fear
to shrink *and* seek to be made plain,
openly to own
both the mists smoking from pure
stone-cold lake-still sun-sweetened places
and the dank mist that rises
from the long-unsunned, sour
pools, hid even from the storm's sluices.

Enduring is the word with *clean*.
The fear once won
of sunward love, it proves – not boulderstone,
baldness, slowly in fire consuming – but green
with life, moss, cup-rock-water, cliff riven
for a springing pine;
and thus, trusted to fire, drawn
towards an enduring sun.

Controversy

They licked the salt at their lip-edge
and fixed how to feed, sleeping on it
and sweating, and went blind
into the flesh. And some god
you say is God says, "That lot's lost"
and rolls them loose
like water on silky dust
rolling away (and if some sparrows
     dropt by and pecked at water globules –
     your god keeps accounts, of
     them and their drinks there?)
...centuries gone...neither here nor there...
done for...("Shove off then").

Judgment? Not His. It's gaming
with loaded dice, & a god made like men
or men with power behind their couldn't-care-less,
and *not* the Truth with the
bite of final cold, & marvelling in it
of bleeding, and waiting, and joy.

A Story

Where *were* you then?
        At the beach.
With your crowd again.
Trailing around, open
to whatever's going. Which one's
calling for you tonight?
        Nobody.
I'm sorry I talk so. Young
is young. I ought to remember
and let you go and be glad.
        No. It's all right.
        I'd just sooner stay home.
You're not sick? did you
get too much sun? a crowd,
I never have liked it, safety in numbers
indeed!
        – He was alone.
Who was alone?
        The one
        out on the water, telling
        something. He sat in the boat that
        they shoved out for him, and told
        us things. We all just stood there
        about an hour. Nobody
        shoving. I couldn't see
        very clearly, but I listened
        the same as the rest.
What was it about?
        About a giant, sort of.
        No. No baby-book giant.
        But about a man. I think –
You *are* all right?
        Of course.
Then tell me
so I can follow. You all
standing there, getting up

out of the beach-towels and gathering
out of the cars, and the ones
half-dressed, not even caring –
    Yes. Because the ones
    who started to crowd around were
    so still. You couldn't
    help wondering. And it spread.
    And then when I would have felt out of it
    he got the boat, and I could
    see the white, a little, and
    hear him, word by word.
What did he tell the lot of you
to make you stand? Politics?
Preaching? You can't believe everything
they tell you, remember –
    No. More, well, a
    fable. Honestly, I –
I won't keep interrupting.
I'd really like you to tell.
Tell me. I won't say anything.
    It is a story. But
    only one man comes.
    Tall, sunburnt, coming
    not hurried, but as though
    there was so much power in reserve
    that walking all day and night
    would be lovelier than sleeping if
    sleeping meant missing it, easy
    and alive, and out there.
Where was it?
    On a kind of clamshell back.
    I mean country, like round about here,
    but his tallness, as he walked there
    made green and rock-grey and brown
    his floorway. And sky a brightness.
What was he doing? Just walking?
    No. Now it sounds strange
    but it wasn't, to hear.
    He was casting seed,
    only everywhere.
    On the roadway, out

on the baldest stone,
on the tussocky waste
and in pockets of loam.
Seed? A farmer?
A gardener rather
but there was nothing
like garden, mother.
Only the queer
dark way he went
and the star-shine of
the seed he spent.
(Seed you could see that way –)
In showers. His fingers
shed, like the gold
of blowing autumnal
woods in the wild.
He carried no wallet
or pouch or sack,
but clouds of birds followed
to buffet and peck
on the road. And the rock
sprouted new blades
and thistle and stalk
matted in, and the birds
ran threading the tall grasses
lush and fine
in the pockets of deep earth –
You mean, in time
he left, and you saw
this happen?
The hollow
air scalded with sun.
The first blades went sallow
and dried, and the one
who had walked, had only
the choked-weed patches
and a few thin files
of windily, sunnily
searching thirsty ones
for his garden

  in all that place.
  But they flowered, and shed
  their strange heart's force
  in that wondering wilderness –
Where is he now?
  The gardener?
No. The story-teller
out on the water?
  He is alone.

  Perhaps a few
  who beached the boat and
  stayed, would know.

The Store Seeds

The seeds   sorted in bins
clean   strange   and plain
under sagging tarpaulins
sifted   several   fine

shifting as the scoop tilts
or the bins are sloped
walled off from loams   rain silt
the darkness that corrupts

in grocery shoals here
or in paper parcelled
for water   pot   and fire
or cupboarded   dry bottled:

the seeds that lie   go
down   go under   go in
go on.   However slow
the   encompassing.

A *Child: Marginalia on an Epigraph*

(Mt. 18:3; *Lk.* 9:48*)*

Small, then, surprised altogether,
helpless, but carried, he is
soon able to cram down, gulp in, trembling with hunger
feeding (no need to name the food, or find it)
or browsing on poison-berries (weep
because birds have eaten the crumbs
marking the trail
homewards) (in the woods, weeping).

Clothed, he is careless of clothing,
he plays till white is grey and black is dusty,
falling and fighting and fish-hooked
and torn and growing and wearing
things, and waiting
to strip off shoes and socks in the
first light of the new world of April's
first grass (the old
wind stirs, and passes).

Safe, at night,
in the deeps of the night-watch kept,
in the clean place,
strange but trusted, as a pool among
cedars in autumn,
leaf-stained, gorgeous, far, deep,
prepared for a tired
child.

Sometimes in murk sleep-ridden
dreading white-eyelashed-night,
the earl king, changeling,
blind horse, mad rider:
bound hand and foot
and mute

but icy music rising
out of the casketed heart
the stolen jewel crying
on the long night wind.

New day, new life time:
"Hey!–Bri-an"
(into the grass-ripe wind
down branch-swept coolness, the
courts of summer's morning)
"Hey!...Bri-an....
Whose side am I on?"
(Wind-snatched pebble-rubber
mock-socker-ball in
play all the while)–
    "On *our* side!"
(just in time for a
somersault celebrating a
long clean punt, clean out from under
the mock-enemy's boot.)

On the festal day (long promised) he
wakes to ice-cream-flavoured air; he possesses
the polka-dot, strut-singing, wave-suds, winking
wonder of off and out to
roads, to a ferry crossing, to
shadows of clouds and sea-gulls afloat, to
rainbows in salty sand that smells of drydock cement –
and the smell clings to fingers and knees –
to bobbling, butterfly-flotsam
crowds, flowing in and coursing
under the gate: the flags,
the white-painted poles, the mealy
sawdust and straw and weed-cracked drought-withered
path-smooth flaking
corners and eavesdropping
silent sunny places
around the edges, before the
waves of attention heap up and ride round and
break in clapping and laughter and you

(Lord!) don't know where to look
for being here
and for joy.

He is completely absorbed
and his heart therefore aches
(radiant, bone-barred):
and to long for the
not enough out of the light yet
to be filled,
fullness.

The Absorbed

The sun has not absorbed
this icy day, and this day's industry – in
behind glass – hasn't the blue and gold, cold
outside. Though not absorbing, this
sought that:

    sheeted, steely, vaulted,
    all gleam, this morning;
    bright blue with one stained wing in the
       northeast, at lunch hour;
    in early afternoon
    abruptly a dust-flurry,
       all but this private coign of place
       deafened, all winding in one cloth of moth.
    Then space breathed, hollowing twilight
       on ice and the pale-grey, pale-blue,
       and far fur-coloured wooden trees
       and ornamental trees.

Towards sundown
a boy came with an aluminum toboggan.
He worked his way, absorbed,
past footmark pocks, on crust,
up ice-ridge, sometimes bumping
down to the Japanese yews, sometimes
scooter-shoving athwart the hill,
then, with a stake,
kneeling,
he paddles, thrusting, speed-wise, then
stabbing, uphill; then
dangling the rope and poring on
slope-sheen, standing, he stashes
the aluminum, upright, in a frost-lumpy shoal

and beside coasting motorcars and parked cars
listens... and off again, toque to the eyebrows,
alone still in the engulfing dark.

The inside breathing here
closes down all the window but a visor-slit
on the night glare.
                 New cold is
in dry-thorn nostrils.

Alone, he plays, still there. We
struggle, our animal fires
pitted against those
several grape-white stars,
their silence.

For Tinkers Who Travel on Foot

What if it *was* a
verse in the
Epistle to the Hebrews that
kept Bunyan
at concert pitch through
deaf and dumb months?
He found
resonance.
He stuck it out till then, too:
not for one instant sure it
would come to anything, in all his
mute madness, nor ever
diverted for one instant.

"On the one hand" – *N.B.*
    "he was difficult" –
his wife, loyal, was, and no wonder,
hysterical.

On the other hand though – N.B. –
when the sky was
finally sundered with glory
and the cornet
rang out, created stillness,

    he knew it, instantly.
He consented, himself, to
the finality of
an event.

The Earth That Falls Away

"Can a man die? Ay, as the sun doth set:
It is the earth that falls away from light."
    –Beddoes, *Death's Jest-Book* II, ii, 39-40

The Roman soldiers' voices
spoke, never hoping
to be heard.
Speech? An unsoldierly interlude
at ease after marching
at bivouac
late, when the night guard
feel alone.

But in that night in that courtyard
they hear the silence
(the ancient voices:
"Hide not thy face far from me")
(the voice of Nehemiah:
"Let thine eyes now be open").

THE BLINDFOLD

I

Brine-crusted, thread-knobbed,
odd-shaped scrap,
clay-soaked, wadded crooked,
rag, however many hours lap and listen
dayshine and dark, across the
children's and the thousand grandsires' morning, an
almost endless history
breaking, broken, over and over,
they cannot distance this
caked pennant or
tuft or
wherever it was ripped....

II

"A bullet blinded me," he said.
"I wouldn't have believed,
those first black weeks, how I would live.
We've married since then. Children. Bread.
Home I never saw indeed
nor needed to. The doctors left
a hope I might recover yet
on file – if nerve and tissue knit –
'Theory' I thought. 'I'm not relieved
to be told the light's not dead
just hibernating, for me (for good).
It's winter where I live.
I've had a northern summer, that
is more than some, let's leave it
at that' – I said."

III

I too have taken it up
from between the warm smooth linens
in the dark, and felt the scorched edges.
I have stood in the empty warehouse turning it
in my fingers helplessly.
By broken panes, patched with cardboard and
weather-sealed with creasey plastics
on sills, did you find the frayed,
smudged wick-end, the
trace? mouldering and
dry, and
damning?

IV

Dawson City Centenary Find:
LIBRARIES...SCHOLARS...AUCTION AGENTS...
IN A GOLD RUSH SHACK (ALL THE INGREDIENTS
OF ROMANCE): first editions
(Renaissance) marginal revisions
of prime importance perhaps, boxed
by long-dead owner, leaves slightly foxed.
Canadiana rare and unique.
A 'Roman History.' A Grammar (Greek)
with a Dame's Academy drawn on the fly-leaf –
calf-bound, with clasps. A little pile of
manuscript notes from the early days,
maps, sketches. On display
with photographs of the Dawson City
member, Centenary Committee,
who found the shack and raised the board
and uncovered this strange anonymous hoard."
WHO WAS THE SCHOLAR OF THE NORTH?
Nobody seems to know. The worth
of this treasure, as specialists unfold
its significance, will exceed, we are told,
all the gold in the hills the original owner
climbed and prospected in, and lies under.

v

The cloth, or part, or
one like it, or a
fetish?
   I see
   the webbed stuff, to which adheres a
   stiff, grey-white, staining substance.
   That which I see I cannot
   touch, or produce in a
   forensic laboratory
   or explain, why it is so small and
   off-square in shape, and open-woven
   as if for a florist's form, or a greenhouse packer's
   shed, for crating, for air freight, to seal out
   ice and time.
I wrap around my knuckles
as I walk, a
cloth – in my pocket finding it
ready. I hear you
describing that wick of ancient
webbing. (In my pockets
it wrings my knuckles.)
   Cloth. Man-made stuff, man-symbol:
   on the forlornest marshland
   of wind-raked nowhere, one
   torn sleeve, striped shirting, ravelled wool,
   sodden, still-folded handkerchief,
   sailcloth.
   Always the bit of cloth, or the rippling bolt at the drygoods
   displaying texture and dyes, sounding
   a muffled thunder in the glassed-in sunlight....

VI

"They did operate, though.
The tissue did begin
to form again. I know
I found out, waiting, how
I had hoped, though
it would have been a sin
to let myself, till then."

VII

Who makes fabrics – ? Nobody
now. Chemists and great
plate-steel gnashing bricked-and-glassed-in places
I guess maybe. You
come right down to it, a cloth,
a piece of cloth, is
another form of the same bits –
electrons, atoms – whatever-you-call-ems-tomorrow (when they
reassemble, reform them in the next
break-
through) –
. . . And to say to me it's always
man-symbol: that has no
mother-naked truth about it. I am
not afraid of your
cloth in my eyes and on
my lips and tongue –

VIII

A hoard? A treasure? The fine
voice from the hill over Dawson City
wanders across dayblue, daygreen:
I remember of course. His books. A pity. . . .

IX

On your gritty Sunday walk, all
the skied ecclesiastical shine
is cold as a music-store trumpet. There is
nothing soft-bodied abroad.
No sails in the Bay. Even the children in automobiles
no longer tug and wrestle with
Navaho-burnt-orange motoring rugs.
In suddenly deaf sidestreets
you find the timeless children
playing, the game of
face-hiding "it," steal-away-All
(and in a parked car
the two-year-old ducking and peering:
not-seeing-grannie-not-there).
    There is screaming in blind man's buff.

X

My dad was blinded
in the war.
Hospitals aren't for
children visiting. I hate it,
having him in there. They are
going to take off his bandage
today. I hope it
worked. I tried
for real, being blind.
About two minutes. It bled
black like, all *at* me.
I couldn't bear it
even two minutes. I guess I don't care. How would it
help if I could be good?
The hospital
keeps us out on account of their rule about children.

XI

Snowflakes cast moth-shadows
on snowdrifts under snow-candled light-standards.
Eyelash brush of snow follows
in the foldaway shadows
between the lamps. And beyond
in the sky-dark a shed
pallor of night waits for an
uptilt-faced, flying
creature, its eye-curves
soft-lashed, soundlessly wide-eyed,
upsweeping, staring into night.
(Do not blink, loving, terrifying night-face,
swerve up into charred snow
forth where we dare not,
falterless, fathom the enfolding depths.)

XII

On the cleared farm
they called
her Sol a scholar
and said he was always a bookworm
and never could learn
rough ways (the way our
men learn them – the tall
dawn-times, stone-blind with cold
and tiring, tiring out, not daring
to be tired, ever,
all our survival
dragging them down). And she'd learn
to ease Sol off, and still warn
the children. While he wore
his eyes out, alone. (Whiskey-blear
muttered the son who became a wanderer
and, some say, a prospector
out Dawson City way.)

XIII

Everywhere I look I see emptiness.
Some snow still has not melted, black
edging black water-sheeted sidewalk-squares
that blank you as you watch and walk and wait.
Only one person knows my name.
An empty telephone box shines in the street
and I gulp at that emptiness and I
am there, silent. I
dial, and lean, nameless, needy
and listen. No word. Find
another coin and dial. And wait.
It rings. rings. rings. Nobody
hears me.
"His eyes behold," the Psalmist said, "His eyelids try...."

XIV

I knew how to live
by hearing and touch
and sense of place. I could pre-judge
obstacles too: at first the couch,
lamp, table; you have to have
them mapped in your mind – you clutch
notions, till you trust sense. Then I could move
out among trees and traffic, a march
in no man's land to risk it, a dive
into invisible interdependence, no crutch
needed, for all the dread. I knew how to live.
Please. Leave me alone.
Bandage my eyes again.
The dream of seeing
I want, as it has been, open
daybreak blue, with the sting
of the far-off; not this urging
of person, colour, thing.
Unclutter me. Relieve
me of this visible. Give
back my sealed-off dayshine....

XV

The broken prism of noise,
pure air (in buildings), pour
of night-wind on a choir of
loosed, elbowing, lift-looney shelters,
traffic-sift, wall-tower,
echo-chambers and hoo-ing
scattering street-boys in the pursuing
murmur haunted stillness, city's unquiet,
the flipped flight
of park pigeons, heavy with knowing
tame food and kicked wing-flop, brewing
in-cringing crowds: Who broke it
in words, fire-pure?
on lips wine-bright?
so that night was in clear
oases lit, not a smoky flare,
no illusory gleam-and-gone?

Your beauty and holiness,
Your fair-seeing, scald.

In the intolerable hour
our fingers and fists
blunder for blindfolds
to have you in our power!

"He does not resist you,"
said James
looking to
Him who, in his hour,
comes.

Branches

The diseased elms are lashing
the hollowing vaults of air.
In movie-washroom-mirrors
wan selves, echoing, stare.

O Light that blinded Saul,
blacked out Damascus noon, *(nonce)*
Toronto's whistling sunset has
a pale, disheartened shine.

If, like a squalling child
we struggled, craving, who
would hear wholeheartedness
and make the world come true?

In ancient date-palm tasselled
summer, King David knew.
Thus seeds could continue splitting
and oceans rolling blue.

The cinnamon carnation
blows funeral incense here.
In darkness is a narcotic,
a last rite, silenced care.

Can *this* kind of blanking
bring us to our knees?
Christ, the soldiers blindfolded you
and slapped mouth and teeth

asking you "Who?"
and nothing was said.
You knew.
And knew they needed bread.

The elms, black-worked on green,
rich in the rich old day
signal wordlessness
plumed along the Dark's way.

Stray selves crowding for light
make light of the heart's gall
and, fly-by-night, would light on
the Light that blinded Saul.

But he died once only
and lives bright, holy, now,
hanging the cherried heart of love
on this world's charring bough.

Wondering, one by one:
"Gather. Be glad."
We scatter to tell what the root
and where life is made.

Miniature Biography of One of My Father's Friends Who Died a Generation Ago

You, sovereign, Lord, have let this be,
Love's gesture here on earth to me.

Your touch would prove all.
Shall I fear it, who want your approval?

My friend's sorrow
I cannot endure. Our
shrinking is your pain.

Let Love's word speak plain.

In Truth

"The fact of a dead
face will never fade
into any beauty-bathed
grove of imagined shadow:
Island, jewelled Esplanade,
City – in earth or ocean bed."

The largeness of mourning,
grief for the known face,
shed an aptitude
for nothing unless certitude.

"I cannot believe
in harps, jasper…"
(hesitantly, as if pitying
one who may still be on
stilts, and the earth shaken).

*

Come, quietness, to the man
love-wrung and turbulent
and alone.

Come, largeness,
to the man anticipating sorrow
and motionless.

Words are too many. In this place
loss is torn –
a vividness
lost, out of the sun.

*

To your apple eyes
shining, in the day
this page, here open, lies
in your way:

Another's eyes
look now, and say,
one stone-dead face
lived, is, will be:

saw those in prison first,
rose, spoke with his
lost friends,
ate honeycomb, and fish.

Though no words but his
speak, in that airlessness,
who hears them is
roused to the utterance

& who trusts him in this
learns all, past time: a voice
no deafness drowns, at last
Love, a face.

*

("Gemmed Palace? Marble Island?
Cathedral under the Sea?
These are the dark blood's dream.
My being would listen
to Him.")

First

Excessive gladness can drag
the 3-dimensional uncircumferenced circle
out of its sublime true
unless contrition also past all bound
extend it.

In the mathematics of God
there are percentages beyond one hundred.

His new creation is
One, whole, and a
beginning.

Person

Sheepfold and hill lie
under open sky.

This door that is "I AM"
seemed to seal my tomb
my ceilinged cell
(not enclosed earth, or hill)

there was no knob, or hinge.
A skied stonehenge
unroofed the prison?
and lo its walls uprising,
very stone drawing breath?

They closed again. Beneath
steel tiers, all walled, I lay
barred, every way.

"I am." The door
was flesh; was there.

No hinges swing, no latch
lifts. Nothing moves. But such
is love, the captive may
in blindness find the way:

In all his heaviness, he passes *through*.

So drenched with Being and created new
the flock is folded close, and free
to feed – His cropping clay, His earth –
and to the woolly, willing bunt-head, forth
shining, unseen, draws near
the Morning Star.

146

...*Person* OR
A Hymn on and to the Holy Ghost

OR To "know God's will"

How should I find speech
to you, the self-effacing
whose other self was seen
alone by the only one,

to you whose self-knowing
is perfect, known to him,
seeing him only, loving
with him, yourself unseen?

Let the one you show me
ask you, for me,
you, all but lost in
the one in three,

to lead *my* self, effaced
in the known Light,
to be in him released
from facelessness,

so that where you
(unseen, unguessed, liable
to grievous hurt) would go
I may show him visible.

Five Breaks

I

Top-spun, swiftly
paid out,
you flung me, dancing, humming:
    "Joy it is
    to ride the day,
    lest that one toy with
    God's play."
The stranger motif here
stunned my now dizzying ear,
and stilled, I lay
toppled and listening.

II

No-one at slack but
jerking guy-ropes or (Look out!)
lash-tackle will
entangle.
Rope-burned, wind-sifted,
praising the Stranger courage and
barrenlands beauty,
strong in your buffeting, I
stood, speed-blind, among
your synchronizing glories.

III

O, then, a careful face
shone bare. In your
held breath, new pinpointed –
were they besiegers' eye-prongs circling
as though a City's famine could be succulence?
I swellingly knew
the aliens, close: all the
my-minded versions of your glory
(like seeing death, life, as your
memoranda left on the blotter
for my day's work; like
chronologies – of "mercies" – these,
these, as if exacted; like
feeling the flesh as tomb
stoned by its own
funereal pieties,
braced for rotting geologies of endurance –
and after that for grubbing,
engine-heat, the
firebird cycle. . . .)

IV

Valentine cards
In the February lace of daylight
through window and doorway glass:
store; children; love; a lakeblue sudsbright
eleven o'clock outdoors, seen too
by the scorched eyes of grief,
the graveled eyes of
utter disappointment, these
zero in the
arrowing sunburst, cone-tip, the
transfixing life.

V

Your tireless rise, your daybreak,
o, here, touch home.

The Word

"*Forsaking all*" – You mean
head over heels, for good,
for ever, call of the depths
of the All – the heart of one
who creates all, at every
moment, newly – for
you do so – and
to me, far fallen in the
ashheaps of my
false-making, burnt-out self and in the
hosed-down rubble of what my furors
gutted, or sooted all
around me – you implore
me to so fall
in Love, and fall anew in
ever-new depths of skyward Love till every
capillary of your universe
throbs with your rivering fire?

"*Forsaking all*" – Your voice
never falters, and yet,
unsealing day out of a
darkness none ever knew
in full but you,
you spoke that word, closing on it forever:
"Why hast Thou forsaken…?"

This measure of your being all-out, and
meaning it, made you
put it all on the line
we, humanly, wanted to draw – at
having you teacher only, or
popular spokesman only, or
doctor or simply a source of sanity
for us, distracted, or only
the one who could wholeheartedly

rejoice with us, and know
our tears, our flickering time, and
stand with us.

But to make it head over heels
yielding, all the way,
you had to die for us.
The line we drew, you crossed,
and cross out, wholly forget,
at the faintest stirring of what
you know is love, is One
whose name has been, and is
and will be, the
I AM.

The Dumbfounding

Jesus the Christ

When you walked here,
took skin, muscle, hair,
eyes, larynx, we
withheld all honour: "His house is clay,
how can he tell us of his far country?"

Your not-familiar pace
in flesh, across the waves,
woke only our distrust.
Twice-torn we cried "A ghost"
and only on our planks counted you fast.

Dust wet with your spittle
cleared mortal trouble.
We called you a blasphemer,
a devil-tamer.

The evening you spoke of going away
we could not stay.
All legions massed. You had to wash, and rise,
alone, and face
out of the light, for us.

You died.
We said,
"The worst is true, our bliss
has come to this."

When you were seen by men
in holy flesh again
we hoped so despairingly for such report
we closed their windpipes for it.

Now you have sought
and seek, in all our ways, all thoughts,
streets, musics – and we make of these a din
trying to lock you out, or in,
to be intent. And dying.

Yet you are
constant and sure,
the all-lovely, all-men's-way
to that far country.

Winning one, you again
all ways would begin
life: to make new
flesh, to empower
the weak in nature
to restore
or stay the sufferer;

lead through the garden to
trash, rubble, hill,
where, the outcast's outcast, you
sound dark's uttermost, strangely light-brimming, until
time be full.

Searching and Sounding

In July this early sky is
a slope-field, a tangled
shining–blue-green, moist, in
heaped up pea-vines, in milk-hidden
tendrils, in light so strong
it seems a shadow of
further light, were the heart
large enough to find its succulence
and feed and not be glutted there.

I look for you
who only know the
melding and the forming of such heart,

and find you here
in the sour air
of a morning-after rooming-house hall-bedroom;
not in Gethsemane's grass, perfumed with prayer,
but here,
seeking to cool the grey-stubbled cheek
    and the filth-choked throat
    and the scalding self-loathing heart, and
failing, for he is
sick,
for I...

I run from you to
the blinding blue of the
loveliness of this wasting
morning, and know
it is only with you
I can find the fields of brilliance
to burn out the sockets of the eyes that want no
weeping
though I am he
            or I am
a babbling boy

aged twenty, mentally distracted, blunted
by sedatives and too-long innocence
without your hand teaching his the ax-heft or
    throttle-bar or
        grease-monkey's gun or
            any craft or art.

And as I run I cry
"But I need something human,
somebody now, here, with me."
Running from you.
The sunlight is sundered by cloud-mass.

My heart is sore, as its
bricked-in ovens smoulder,
for I know whose hand at my elbow
I fling from me as I run.

But you have come and sounded
a music around me, newly,

as though you can clear
all tears from our eyes only
if we sound the wells of weeping with
another's heart, and hear
another's music only.

Lord, the light deepens as the
summer day goes down
in lakes of stillness.
Dwarf that I am, and spent,
touch my wet face with
the little light I can bear now, to mirror,
and keep me
close, into sleeping.

                *

From the pearl and grey of daybreak
you have brought me to
sandstone, baldness, the place
of jackals, the sparrow's skull,

tumbled skeletons of what were
hills clothed in forest
and spongy meadows, the place of
baked stone, dryness, famine,
of howling among the tombs.

   From the first dews, the
      grasses at their budding,
         fragrance of mountain snow
           and sunfat cedars
to the farthest reaches
where your Descent began, on the beach gravel
ground by sea-slimed teeth...
those bloodless horses....

To what strange fruits in
the ocean's orchards?

Reaching
with Light that is perfect, needed no
    kernels to swell nor juices to syrop nor
    no further making – *all* newness –
    all being
that the remotest fishrib,
the hairiest pink-thing there
might as one fragment
make towards the fullness you
put off, there, on the
ravening shore I view, from
my gull-blanched cliffs,
and shiver.
GATHER my fragments towards
the radium, the
all-swallowing moment
once more.

A Prayer Answered by Prayer

My heart was on my sleeve,
I knew it, barely warm:
"This was what I believe,
How can I hold firm?"

On a flat earth, solid
I stand "upright" and stare
at sunset's moon-globe pallid
in a skied nowhere.

What only Christ makes real
rests in astonishment
in one Uncommonweal.
Love is heart-rent.

"All-creating Son
whose badge I thought to wear,
where you have found me, burn
me, your beacon fire."

For Dr. and Mrs. Dresser

Your doctor, Lord,
from West Irian,
brought pictures of a leaf that served as plate,
and grubs, fat, silkily hirsute, that men
need there for nourishment.
Whoever speak your word
along that coast must share
that feast of fatness first
for love of you and them
who offer from your provenance their best.
The gorge that finds your natural good
in food that squirms is
given aptitude, surely, by grace. . . .

As that doctor, Lord,
learned to subsist, in order
to love first-hand, for you, and tell
how God, to His plain table
invites them too, and will
dwell among them who offer Him their all,
You, once for all,
offered and dwelt – you, fairest beyond call
                of mortal imagining:
here, taking on yourself not only
our spoiled flesh, but the lonely
rot of the rebel, of the solitary,
of all not-God on earth, for all
who claim, in all your range of time. And still
without one queasy tremor, you could wholly
swallow our death, take on our
lumpish wingless being, darkened out
to cold and night – except for
the timeless love
even for us, my Lord.
And having suffered us to glut
the pure well-spring, and having

plumbed even hell, for us, you could
come back, in flesh, living, and
open out the shaft and sweep
of clarity and scope,
flooding us with your risen radiance,
can bid us, now, in turn, o gentle Saviour:
"take, eat –
live."

The Christian's Year in Miniature

I

Beside the still waters,
infant-pure,
God is, in flesh.
Now the skies soar

with song. Heaven utters.
In a white blur
lost, in a rush
caught up, we hear

II

To the hills we lifted
our eyes, and you
sat on the pasture ridge
strongly in view,

and taught us. The breeze wafted
your voice through and through
our hearts. From the timeless verge
you moved, to our *now*.

III

Unsullied one, though midnight
is lucid to your heart,
here, in God's unspeaking
you are set apart.

Where kings brought gold by starlight
at first, now I have marred
your clarity, breaking
my clayfull–to your hurt.

IV

A walnut shell broken
(small, wafered skull)
still litters the hillside.
Morning breaks, still.
The garden, awaking
to a terrible day-swell
knows the rock-sweet, the pulse-set
of Emmanuel.

V

Your places of dwelling
held up for our own
together, if we fashion
your *now* with *soon*

fill us with spoiling
of the deaths we had won.
Only in your possession
can such Life go on.

Of Tyranny, in One Breath

(translated from a Hungarian poem by Gyula Illyes, 1956)

Where tyranny sets in
it settles in
not only with bren guns
not only in prisons

in police questioning,
night-shouts echoing
(armed guard or sentry)
for there is tyranny

not only in smoke-griming
flared-up accusation –
nor in confession –
wall-tapping in prison –

not only in the cursory judge's decision:
GUILTY –
not only is tyranny
in the military

crackle: "Attention...Fire!"
nor in the tired
rattle of drums, nor the twitch
of the corpse to the ditch,

not only in the
hinge creaking ajar
for hurried news in a
half-whisper

nor the "Psst!" with a finger
to lip, not only where
faces are blank, shuttered in
is tyranny – and behind

the gasping scream
caught but still flopping,
in a silence thickened by
mute tears flooding
and the eyes throbbing –

tyranny is not only in
the standing, standing,
the cheering, the chanting,

where it sets in
it spreads and settles not only
in the clapping till the palms sting,
in the opera's trumpetings

in the park statuary
where every stone shouts hurray,
in the art museums
in the paint in the frames

or in particular
in the brush that painted there;

not only in the night, the flow
of a sleek car, its purr,
nor how
it draws up at the door;

where tyranny settles in
it soaks in,
a presence in all there is
more than your childhood's God was

for tyranny is
in the nursery schools
in a father's advice
on a mother's face

in how a youngster guardedly
answers a strange passerby,

not only in barbed wire,
the book-rows the censor
smiled on, or worse than these
the deadening officialese,

for tyranny is
in the good-bye kiss,
in how a wife says to her man
"When will you be home?"

not only in the dull
"how are you's" in the street
or the chill
when a handshake goes limp

or your girl's face suddenly
freezing over
because it is there when you
come together

not only in interrogating
not only in the response you're making
suddenly, aswim in talk
like wine where flies get stuck,

its Presence haunts
even your dreams,
It's in the marriage bed – before
that, in the desire

for you crave only to caress
the loveliness It first possessed,
with It you lay when you believed
you loved,

It is on tumbler and plate
in nostrils and throat
in the day's chill outdoors
in the dark corridors

in a room with the windows wide
as if sweet death rotted outside,
in a sealed house
like leaking gas

to your thought's faltering words, It
adds the "or" and "but,"
in your imagination even
your hear It breathing:

the Milky Way is now
a searchlight raking through
night's minefield; and star-glint
a Judas-slot

or heaven aswarm with glimmering lamps
one universal labour camp,
for tyranny can speak from
confessional, carillon,

through the priest or maniac–
parliament, pulpit, penal rack
are alike boards where It can strut,
with your eyes open, shut,

It eyes you still
like a disease
deep-seated as memories,

the trainwheels rattle "caught...
captured...captive...caught"
on mountainside, by the shore
It fills the air

crackles in lightning–shocks
in unexpected creaks,
light-flickers–It starts
with your lurching heart,

in clockticking quiet
in boredom's caged unquiet
in a colonnading downpour's
prison bars

in a dingy-white snowfall's
prison walls,
through your dog's eyes
It looks at you, because

It is everywhere before you
It is in your tomorrow,
in what you think,
work at, eat & drink,

by following where It led
you've shaped Its riverbed,
if you peer out, a gazing-ball
shows Its mirrored eyes on you

watching, – you might run? but *you*
are the prison bars you're staring through,
into your pipe smoke coiling
into your clothes congealing

It sucks and lops and licks Its chops
and gnaws your bone,
you fumble to think. . . . Its thought
kneads at your brain,

your eye no longer sees
for Its fantasies,

a forest-fire, flames
raging – and you blame
one match not out, let fall –
now, past control, It's on
field, factory, home,

you don't know any more
what meat and bread are for,
what desire was like, love,
what it meant to live,

the servile whom It tutors
fits on his own fetters,
eating, you fatten It,
Its is the child that you beget,

your spittle tastes of It, your skin
oozes It, It slimes within,
you are not you, but It—

like moles we fumble in the sun,
dark our only home,
Sahara or a cell
would serve as well,

for where It is, all's vile,
nothing's worthwhile...
not this song, however true,
nothing you do

It stands above
your waiting grave,
It tells who you have been,
your dust will serve Its ends.

Report from the Pedestrians' Outpost

The leaf lettuce
is not from Texas but the
steel in the gullet,
pig-iron-tasting tongue
is not from Steep Rock.

The cottagers in moving files
coupéd now, fend off
the elements with chrome trim;
even in the autumn rain
their furs are dry, their notched
lapels lie flat.
The fish-cold newsboy handles
wet dimes.
In lonely places
the lichen soaks,
turns leathery as kelp;
and shingles comb
the rivering rainfall,
shining north north-east.

The vows of the Pheasant
hollow the cylinder-sheen of
sleep.
Daylight comes crested with
fantastic ornaments.

Along the streets, Yip, Yip,
the beggars are coming.

A Sad Song

I

The young catalpa
tree on Robert Street
sickens. Storms
break branches, strip
the crisping leaves, soak
the fake-brick wall-front.

II

It spokes out, forcible
in iron radiance
through snow,
into the winter-blue nights that sing
with cold and star-wash.

III

The sound of its sticks in wind
and its beaten trunk,
the design of its sky-blunted hollowness
form long memory
for the young on Robert Street.

IV

June is now sealed, silent.
Form without springing makes of it
a wrong season,
makes even this perfumed rain
autumnal.

Once

"When earth is cold,
when it turns its shoulder
on the ungrudging sun
pole-tilted into fronting
the eyes of utter dark:

"snow forms and falls, crystals, air-fretted,
in depth wind-shaped, in the light
white, and with a breathing
even by night of, as if,
eyelid pallor.

"The melting, coursing sun
moves (hurting and lilting,
dimming and flashing).
Earth is all pools and all the
waters speak, in the new
sky's language.

"The myths of earth-ferment,
seed-nub in dissolution
spiking up swords of
green, bright under blueness,

"make shy our brutish,
averted, black-drinking, still-
ice-splintered
eyes."

Lonely Lover

Lit smudge fires
white fog and frost killing cherry trees
tears clear in the under clapboard dark cheeks tallow
all things tearsized going into the
peacock eyes of the dark here
the chill the waiting
with the white flesh cherished before the flower in
curled woe.

There is a musty smell of dear old nail-clasped thong-buckled
saddle-rubbed beautiful
Renaissance albums.

The words cherished forgotten but
one aching still towards
Christian brightness and
unmourning;
still the smudges wink.

In Eporphyrial Harness

Hill-hoe
till the liberal varnish, the
daze-sun go
down and the pin-
        flare-
        finish
        star-bright
become alltoday, furnish
us sun (eyes) (ice).

Janitor Working on Threshold

Boot-soles and overalled haunches to the street,
kneeling –
bowed from the ivy-falling, darkly-bright
day-ceiling,
and from cool stone, green court inside –
prising some broken stripping loose, and all in
slow skill, plain sight,
working, till no one need be afraid of falling –

    this street
    and door in the final stilling
    of all (of the one at the threshold with the rest)
    recall the less than the least,
    John, and the wings, and healing.

Bestialities

When I get mad I stamp
sd the ant.

$*$

Sd the mother ladybug if you
know who you are it's
all in that and you may
leave it to the others with their
pads and blast off.

$*$

What are you doing sd the dolphin up a
gumtree eating peanuts:
(swimming?)

$*$

Because it was going to be
autumn the centipede was
sitting at a roadside table snapping
   the 3 buckles on the (each)
     foot's
       galoshes.

$*$

Better not call wings beautiful unless
you're flying with them sd
the dragonfly and then it's better than
wanting toes.

$*$

Sd the mite on the
single page of a sad letter
Eureka.

Canadian/Inverted

Frozen blocks of air –
a flag congealed in one –
triangulated by
tin roofs, splintered
where under-mantle Life whanged on a tree-root,
       nailed earth to sky:
Here I move
       proving
no block of air can stay me
       spiritus.

Walking Behind,
en Route, in Morning, in December

This man is not entirely
,by himself, satisfactory:
he presents first his instep
at each step
allowing too little glimpse
of newboot soles which
with his orange-&-grey hair are
all about him that is not grey
  from behind.
But yet as his topcoat splits at the
unbuttoned slit and
in the wind off the
withered-moss tundra
bellies, one half east, one
south south-east,
I admit that this man, since he is
not by himself, is a
one, is
satisfactory.

Hot June

People are pink-cheekt only
long enough to
ferret out what if we were wan and wiser we
would let
be.

Give us the word and we worry
it out of its soil and run
off with it
        (IN-FORM) between our teeth
and *have at it* and set up a
branch office to
do it for
people.

And o the zeal of thy cheek,
the tired plumes trailing
home!

Dust composes its late sunlight petals, ribbands, metals,
shorelessness.

Natural/Unnatural

Evening tilt makes a
pencil-box of our
street.
The lake, in largeness, grapey blueness
casts back the biscuit-coloured pencil-box, boxes, toys, the
steeple-people, all of it, in one of those
little mirrory shrugs.

The north-east sky too
grows fuselage cool.

On the horizon
ghosts of peeled parsnips point their
noseless faces up,
out; ghost-bodies pile up on each other, all prone, all
pointless, blanking, refusing.

Even the west, beyond the tinged rooftops
smells of cobalt;

    "no–the
    charring of a peeled stick in a bonfire
    is the smell: newness,
    October crackling..."
large pink children have, all the same, sniffed
the ice in
that quirk of sunset
but refuse
fear.

There is still a lingering
sand-edge of sound
darkness explores.

In hope I say: it is a
listening into a
voice-sound, a voice making with silence.

"Hope is a dark place
that does not refuse
fear?"

     True, the natural night is pressure on my ribs:
     despair – to draw that in, to
     deflate the skin-pouch, crunch out the
     structure in one
     luxuriant deep-breathed zero –
     dreamed already, this is
     corruption.

I fear *that*.

I refuse, fearing; in hope.

In a Season of Unemployment

These green painted park benches are
all new. The Park Commissioner had them
planted.
Sparrows go on
having dust baths at the edge of
the park maple's shadow, just where
the bench is cemented down, planted
and then cemented.

   Not a breath moves
   this newspaper.
   I'd rather read it by the Lapland sun at midnight. Here we're
   bricked in early by a
   stifling dark.

On that bench a man in a
pencil-striped white shirt
keeps his head up and steady.

   The newspaper-astronaut says
   "I feel excellent under the condition of weightlessness."
And from his bench a
scatter of black bands in the hollow-air
ray out – too quick for the eye –
and cease.

   "Ground observers watching him on a T.V. circuit said
   At the time of this report he
   was smiling, Moscow ra-
   dio reported."
I glance across at him, and mark that
he is feeling
excellent too, I guess, and
weightless and
"smiling."

Simon: finis

Not the leaf-crisp wind but the
cotton-thin
in a wheat-silvered sky.
Spruce-cones are sieves to the clear
cold, as are cliffs,
shingles, men
in the meadowing day.

Bone rick man on an iron cot
under the singling shingles, high
by sky-light hears a cement-mixer
tumble and grind far off
and is wise.

Salmon-cold hands on the hod and the steady
shoring of hours
humped through a life time
touches him, laid out now in his tatters,
to a gradual smile.

Christmas: Anticipation

For Christmas week the freezing rain
stings and whispers another presence
in the street-lot's unlit needles of wet trees
waiting for Christmas buyers.
The hoar stone
cliff of an unfamiliar church
rises from sidewalk rim off up into
dimming lofts of air;
pigeons flap and chuckle invisibly
up there, when tire-slop and motor-hum
stop, for an odd
moment, and there comes
bird-sound, and the city rain sound falling.

The man newly come home
from university where he was
a freshman, and in love,
slants his face into the smart
of storm, in solitary
pacing, lost from his love, flesh-chilled
by the massive, ornate world that does not matter
because his love is left
out, for tonight and seven more days and nights, and
his heart rocks and swings with the forlorn
lantern of if-daybreak after
heartbreak – the
vision a clam has had –
and it lit him into hope of holiness, a
slit that makes
aching of blindness.

The patient years in the appointed place
brought Zacharias, dumb with unbelieving,
flame-touched, to front
the new sky,
the ancient desert ways

rustling with grasshoppers' thighs, yielding
from dry, spiky places,
wild honey, and a brook starting.

The buyers wedge in doorways
waiting for lights, lifts, taxis.
The boy lonely in love moves with the wind
through electric bright, through fading, light.
The old man with his censer, dazed down the
centuries, rays his
dry-socketed eyes, dimming
still, till he could believe, towards,
with, joy.
Down falling whispers
stir in the lopped firs, waiting.

And Around

A tree its twigs up-ending
November had bared:
drenched in height, brisk with
constellar seed-sprigs, thrusting
its ancient ranginess towards
the cold, the burning, spared
of leaf, sealed in, unbending.

Earth, showering like a sparkler
shedding its growth
plumes it in purpled darkness,
and the tree's barb
rides tinily springward.

Transit

Blowing hard at the bus stop:
south-bound, NW corner.
Barometer falling.
Stars falling, but in that
blue sky who marks it, they fall all over out there.

Wind's off the Barren Straits.
But the sun is blowing too.
Reared high out of the nest
snakeheads flap in it till the
tear ducts crackle.

The whole geste unrolls; black cars,
poles, black & white headlines,
dentist's floss, wire-mesh,
heads spinning, and
a thorn needle for every solitary tune even though there's no
automatic arm. And it's
all plugged in
and everything's coming.
But the bus isn't coming.

Noon keeps swallowing.

A Nameless One

Hot in June a narrow winged
long-elbowed-thread-legged
living insect lived
and died within
the lodgers' second-floor bathroom here.

At 6 A.M.
wafting ceilingward,
no breeze but what it living made there;

at noon standing
still as a constellation of spruce needles
before the moment of
making it, whirling;

at four a
wilted flotsam, cornsilk, on the linoleum:

now that it is
over, I
look with new eyes
upon this room
adequate for one to
be, in.

Its insect-day
has threaded a needle
for me for my eyes dimming
over rips and tears and
thin places.

Urban Tree

An orphan tree
forks for air
among the knees of
clanking panoplied buildings.
Its auburn fernstrings pour
invisible waterthreads of falling life
from the overplastered earth into
the very air-pillars that build that
dove & lamb's wool cloud.
And the loud
wonder of my breath
the tree too angles in, to
further the dark ways of root and loam
even among
subsurface pipes, steel stems, cellars, the drumming
onrush.
In a thin whitish space
off-centre, vast unblur,
the sun lives
as its alive sapling
lives and is traced in
fingering on the
arrested armour here, this
morning.

Unspeakable

The beauty of the unused
  (the wheatear among birds, or
     stonechat)
the unused in houses (as a
  portion of low roof swept by the
    buttery leaves of a pear tree
    where a manx cat is
    discovered – just now – blinking his
      sunned Arctic sea-eyes in the
      sun-play)
the beauty of the
  unused in one I know, of
  excellent indolence
    from season into
      skywide wintering
should be
confidently, as it is
copious and new into the morning,
celebrated.

A Note on the Text

This volume includes the complete, unaltered text of *Winter Sun and other poems* (London: Routledge & Kegan Paul, 1960, and Toronto: The University of Toronto Press, 1960) and *The Dumbfounding* (New York: Norton, 1966). Several poems originally appeared in both volumes; they are printed here as part of *Winter Sun*.

Miss Avison has also published *sunblue* (Hantsport, Nova Scotia: Lancelot Press, 1978).

Acknowledgements

For *Winter Sun*, the author wishes to thank the John Simon Guggenheim Memorial Foundation for a 1956 grant which made possible the ordering of manuscripts and provided leisure for much of the work here. Grateful acknowledgement is also due to the editors of *Combustion* (Toronto); *Kenyon Review; Origin; Poetry* (Chicago); *Queen's Quarterly;* A.J.M. Smith's *The Book of Canadian Poetry* (W.J. Gage), and his *The Oxford Book of Canadian Verse;* and to Ralph Gustafson's *Penguin Book of Canadian Verse* for the poems first published there. For *The Dumbfounding*, the author would like to thank the editors of the following periodicals and anthologies, where some poems in the present volume first appeared: *Blew Ointment; Canadian Review; Ganglia; His; Kenyon Review; Origin; Poetry at Mid-Century; Poetry 62.*

The series The Modern Canadian Poets *presents the finest poetry of contemporary English Canada. Each volume is drawn from the work of a single writer, either at mid-career or after a lifetime's achievement.*

PUBLIS

Date Due